COMBAT RECON

COMBAT

RECON

5th Air Force Images from the SW Pacific 1943-45

ROBERT J. STAVA

Schiffer Military History
Atglen, PA

Design & Art Direction: Robert Stava
Additional Photography: Susan Stava

Library of Congress Catalog Number: 2007932751.

Printed in China.
ISBN: 978-0-7643-2777-3

We are always looking for people to write books on new and related subjects. If you have an idea for a book, please contact us at the address below.

Published by Schiffer Publishing Ltd.
4880 Lower Valley Road
Atglen, PA 19310
Phone: (610) 593-1777
FAX: (610) 593-2002
E-mail: Info@schifferbooks.com.
Visit our web site at: www.schifferbooks.com
Please write for a free catalog.
This book may be purchased from the publisher.
Please include $3.95 postage.
Try your bookstore first.

In Europe, Schiffer books are distributed by:
Bushwood Books
6 Marksbury Ave.
Kew Gardens, Surrey TW9 4JF
England
Phone: 44 (0)20 8392-8585
FAX: 44 (0)20 8392-9876
E-mail: info@bushwoodbooks.co.uk
www.bushwoodbooks.co.uk
Free postage in the UK. Europe: air mail at cost.
Try your bookstore first.

This book is dedicated to
my mother Rochelle,
John H. Stava,
and to all the
men of the 5th Air Force.

CONTENTS

Foreword

The Far East Air Force was renamed the Fifth Air Force in February of 1942. It did not function as an Air Force until Sept., 1942 when General George C. Kenney took over as Commanding General. My outfit, the Third Bomb Group (L), arrived in Brisbane, Australia February 25. I was a member of the 5th Air Force from its inception until I boarded the General A.E. Anderson troop ship on February 18, 1945 to return to the States.

Shortly after Pearl Harbor, President Roosevelt and Prime Minister Churchill made the decision to defeat Germany first. It became very evident to the troops in the S.W. Pacific that the Pacific was to be the step child of WW II. The bulk of men and materiel was sent to the European Theater. We got the hand-me-downs and the leftovers and were left to fight a war with one arm tied behind us. 1942 proved to be extremely costly to the 5th in both men and aircraft.

Case in point: my outfit the Third Bomb Group. On December 7, '41 we consisted of five tactical Sqs.; Hq., 8th, 13th, 89th and the 90th. The 8th was equipped with the A-24 Douglas dive bomber. The other four were equipped with the A-20 Douglas light bomber. In their haste to get us overseas (We left the States seven weeks after Pearl Harbor.), the powers that be failed to provide aircraft for us. On March 10 1942 we arrived at a new air strip at Charters Towers, Queensland, Australia ready to fight a war but had nothing to fight with. In March we received 42 pilots and 64 enlisted men from the 27th Bomb Group in the Philippines along with 24 A-24s. The aircraft were assigned to the 8th Sq., the pilots and enlisted men were spread through out the other Sqs. Also in March we begged, borrowed or stole 25 B-25s from the Dutch that were divided between the 13th and 90th Sq. The 89th went begging for a while.

There were times when we could only put six planes in the air for a mission. Were it not for the borrowed men from the RAAF we would have been hard pressed to man those planes. It was not unusual to lose two or three of those planes to enemy Zeros. May 25, 1942 we sent six (some sources say 8) over Lae on a mission and five of them were shot down. For the next two years there were times when one of the Sqs. would be inactive for the lack of aircraft.

Almost two years after our arrival we finally received a full compliment of A-20s in January, 1944. The Fifth has been known as the "Forgotten Fifth". I've heard the question, why, since we read a lot about them. The reason you read and see more about them to day is two fold.

WW II was not only the greatest armed conflict in the history of mankind - it was also the most documented on film. In the case of the Fifth Air Force each Bombardment Group had some of their bombers equipped with still cameras, When they started a bomb run the camera would make an exposure every three to four seconds on a 150 ft roll of film 9 inches wide. Fifth Bomber Command had a Photo Section with some cinematographers. They would assign one or two of them to a Bombardment Group and they would record the mission on 16 mm movie film. In addition to this an awful lot of the troops carried their own personal cameras. Fellows like me, being in a Photo Section had an additional benefit. We were able to get a lot of the mission photos for our personal collections. Since the coming of computers and the internet (World Wide Web) a lot of these personal collections have found their way onto Websites. Also a lot of the 16 mm movie film has found its way onto documentaries on the History Channel and other channels. The second reason you read and see more is that 60 years after the fact more of the surviving Veterans of the Fifth are opening up and talking about their time in the "Green Hell", which New Guinea was known as by those who served there. The "Forgotten Fifth" refers its war time service - when it was a step child of WW II.

Jack Heyn
Photographer
3rd Bomber Group

January 2006

Introduction

I never met John Stava.

In fact, about the time he disappeared off the family radar - which by all accounts was shortly after my grandfather's funeral in 1954 - my father was barely 13 years old and I wasn't even a remote concept. But I can tell you a few interesting things about him and I can tell you that he's played a pivotal role in my life. If there's one thing I've learned in the process of putting together this book, it's that you can never underestimate the ability of the past, even one you may not be aware of, to reach out and touch the present and maybe even the future.

This whole business started out with a question to my great Aunt Jo whom no-one had spoken to in over twenty years about my family history. That ultimately resulted in a box of photos that hadn't seen the light of day in fifty years being handed to me filled with reels of 16mm color film, medals, papers, and hundreds of photographs that covered my great uncle John Stava's experience in the Southwest Pacific during World War II from 1943-1945.

Sometimes that's where asking questions will get you to. I wasn't even aware that I had a uncle John Stava until I started poking around the family tree back in 1993, and in short order I was able to discover that his life had wound down to a sad end in 1985 in Miami, Florida. I started with a service photo and his VA Record which gave me the bare bones of his service record but little else. I had no idea where to even begin. It would be a few years before I finally received that box of his belongings and found out to my surprise that he had not only participated but extensively documented a fascinating part of world history - the campaign in the Southwest Pacific against the Japanese in WWII.

I quickly discovered that there is not a lot of readily available information on the Southwest Pacific (SWP) campaign. If a glance through our local bookstores are any indication, to the average American the war in the Pacific can probably be summed up by a handful of defining events; the Japanese bombed Pearl Harbor, there was a pivotal battle at Midway, the Marines raised a flag at Iwo Jima and we dropped some atomic bombs on Japan. MacArthur get's plenty of press despite the fact that he spent much of the campaign safely back in Australia (early on in the war he earned the nickname "Dugout" Doug from the troops, but that's a whole other story). Someone paying closer attention might be aware of a bit of business in a place called Guadalcanal, a problem with Kamikaze's in Leyte, and that some mavericks were flying shark mouthed P40's in China. But pretty much zip on the 5th Air Force and the campaign in the SW Pacific. To get info on the 5th you have really start digging around. Even myself, a WWII aviation enthusiast since I was a kid, really knew very little about the war in the South Pacific and next to nothing about the 5th Air Force or what had happened in New Guinea and the Philippines.

What I did know however was that in my hands was a story that would have to be told. The next task was to find out just what that story was.

One of the first people I contacted was Russell Sturzebecker, a 5th AF Veteran and author of "The Roarin' 20's: History of the 312th BG". He asked me if I had ever done anything like this before. When I confessed that I really hadn't, he said; "*Well it's a lot more involved and it's going to take hell of a lot more time than you think - you've got your work cut out for you. You have to get all the facts straight!*"

He wasn't joking.

Photo: Susan Stava

In sorting through the photos what struck me immediately about my uncle's collection was the breadth of subjects it covered. Not just intense combat images, but images of the every day and ordinary of life in the Southwest Pacific theater. With the instincts of a born photojournalist he obsessively photographed everything going on around him. No subject was too ordinary. On top of that he had a talent for composing his subject matter. Combined with best tools available at the time, which meant the best cameras and film available, the result was an impressive collection of high-quality images.

The next task at hand was to catalogue and scan the images, uncover their subject matter and try and sort out the chronology of events they depicted. While some of the photos had his personal notes scripted on them, the majority had no information whatsoever. All I had were endless questions. Who were these people? Where were these pictures taken? And: did he take all photographs himself?

Fortunately that box of belongings included few additional key pieces of information; citation and mission reports, and more importantly, a little black book from the war where he'd collected names and addresses of many of the guys he'd served with.

As far as his taking all the photographs, the answer as it

turned out was, no. In combat the majority of photos from B-25s and A-20's were taken by fixed cameras mounted at the rear of the plan set to take shots a regular intervals as the plane flew over the target. In heavier bombers such as B-17s and B-24s fixed, handheld, and 16mm movie cameras were used depending on the nature of the mission. On occasion crewmen would bring along smaller handheld camera's and take personal photos. So I had to concede that most likely the majority of the combat images were taken by fixed cameras. To make matters more convoluted I was informed by Fred Miller, who worked with my uncle in the photo lab, that often they would make duplicates of any images they processed that struck their interest. Ultimately I decided what was important was not who took what images but the story they told.

Discovering that story has been quite a journey. What started out as a box of photos I knew nothing or little about became a window into a past rich with amazing events. I wound up discovering that my uncle had two different careers within the 5th Air Force. For the first year and a half he was Lab Chief of the 5th Air Force Advanced Echelon Photo Section, which processed all incoming photographs for General Whitehead's Advanced Echelon Headquarters. In addition to his lab duties he would routinely fly recon and combat missions as a photographer and sometimes gunner, despite the fact that wasn't exactly in his job description. I was told that he rarely returned from a mission without having fired his guns. Then, at a time when most of the original photo section personnel were rotating home in late 1944, he transferred into a front line combat position with the 17th Reconnaissance Squadron, which General Whitehead considered as "His boys". He served there as a tail gunner until finally being rotated home in June of 1945. I was able to locate surviving veterans who served with him in the photo lab and get much of the story on what and who the Photo Section was along with some insights into my uncle's character. I was also able to track down veterans from the 17th Reconnaissance Squadron including the pilot he crewed with along with friends and acquaintances from other crews. Meaningless names with photos in the collection suddenly became real people with histories and personalities.

Naturally what also happened was that more than a few interesting side roads wound up getting visited as I spoke with more and more people. I talked several times with Marge Bong Drucker, widow of America's highest scoring ace, Major Dick Bong, and surprised her with a few photos I had of her late husband she had never seen before. I discovered how that photo of her on Major Bong's P-38 came about and that my uncles lab actually provided that enlargement and replacements when needed. I ended up interviewing and corresponding with other 5th Air Force veterans like Garrett Middlebrook, one of the few B-25 strafer pilots to keep daily diaries of his experiences as they unfolded, Vic Tatelman of "Dirty Dora" fame, and many others. The veterans I spoke with provided valuable insights as to how they dealt physically and mentally with fighting a war in the tropics. I spent long hours with yellowed records in the National Archives, corresponded with historians and authors around the globe and even found one Australian Ex-Patriot sitting on his front step right down the street from me. So you could say it's been quite a trip.

Photo: Susan Stava

Still, there are still plenty of mysteries and holes in the story which I have to accept may never be explained. I have four bronze stars out of six in my uncles medals I have no official information on other than that they are pinned on his Asiatic Service Ribbon. I have a stack of letters from his commanding officers heartily recommending him for promotion to Lieutenant, but for reasons unknown the promotion never occurred. I have a citation report indicating that while serving for the 17th Recon in 1945 he flew "long-range photo reconnaissance missions against enemy airdromes, shipping, and ground installations during which photographs were taken which furnished valuable intelligence information" and yet there are almost no photographs in his collection of these missions - all the missions with the 17th Recon he flew as a tail gunner, not as a photographer. And I can only speculate what motivated him to leave a cushy job with the photo section and get transferred into a full time combat squadron on the front lines and what else he might have doing there, amongst other things. At some point you simply accept that many questions will probably always be lying around unanswered, and settle for the contentment that you found as many answers as you did.

So for me the story told here in this book has been twofold: first it's been about discovering a lost family member who vanished over fifty years ago and second it's been about discovering a chapter of history in which an amazing human drama was played out. With that in mind I've expanded the book to include as many of the surrounding events relevant to my uncles wartime experiences. Without straying too far off the road I hope.

The war in the Southwest Pacific took a terrible toll on both sides. Casualties in the New Guinea campaign alone came close to 200,000 including civilians. For the bomber crews of the U.S. Air Force there was plenty of insanity going on there as well. There were pilots skipping thousand pound bombs into enemy ships from mast height. They loaded aircraft up with gun packs and parachute bombs and had them attack airfields at treetop height. They had guys load planes up with bombs and crews and sent them over tropical mountain ranges to navigate through massive tropical thunderstorms that would toss them about like candy - and occasionally slam them into mountains - and then they would have to get to an enemy airbase by dead reckoning, face enemy aircraft and AA fire, turnaround a fly back through it again. Day after day. They had to live with mud, mosquitoes, mold, snakes and leeches.

It was one hell of a way to make a living.

Now to get back to Russell Sturtzbeckers statement. He told me I had to get the facts straight. What he neglected to tell me is that sometimes that can be pretty much impossible. Many incidents related here are like the classic crime scene conundrum: a dozen witnesses will give you a dozen different versions of what happened and somewhere in the middle probably lies the truth. Many times accounts from one veteran contradicted another's or written reports. The same goes for photographs - many images have varying background information depending on the source you're referencing. Sixty-one plus years after these events occurred, it can be an exercise in frustration trying to sort out what really happened and sometimes your best shot is an educated guess.

As for my uncle John, he remains something of an enigma. The shy, quiet man in the background who never told his story, a person defined by a few quick recollections of his peers and family, a man who reveals little about himself. You'll catch glimpses of him throughout this book but by and large his story is told through the pictures he took and collected, the people he met and the history these photographs have captured. John never shared his war experiences with anyone in the family, not even the woman he married in the last ten years of his life, but even so a good part of that story has finally come to light.

John, I've given it my best shot.

I hope you enjoy the images here if nothing else, walk away from this book with a little more insight and understanding with an often overlooked piece of world history.

Robert Stava
New York City
2006

"Always glad to hear from someone interested in the real war in the Pacific, as opposed to that little skirmish they had going in Europe."

-Jack Heyn, 3rd BG
opening interview statement

Background

In the process of researching this book much information has come to light regarding an all but forgotten yet fundamentally important unit of the 5th Air Force.

Various labeled the "5th Air Force Advanced Echelon Photo Section", or "5th AF Advon Photo Lab", this was a unit created in early 1943 by Colonel David W. Hutchison, under direction of General Ennis C. Whitehead, for the express purpose of processing all incoming photographs for 5th Air Force Intelligence. The unit was attached directly to 5th Air Force Advon headquarters under Whitehead and consisted of about 18 to 20 men, many of whom were professional photographers in peacetime. Reports also refer to John Stava as being from "Headquarters and Headquarters Squadron, Advanced Echelon, Fifth Air Force".

The Photo Lab was trained in the States at Lowry Air Force Base in Colorado, assembled at the 5th AF Base located near San Francisco at Pittsburg, California and brought over to Australia in early 1943 where they trained and finalized their operations and procedures at Archerfield in Brisbane. Some of the personal such as my uncle had received additional training at the aerial gunnery school at Laredo AFB in Texas. As the New Guinea campaign progressed the unit was moved from Port Moresby to Nadzab, to Owi, then eventually to the Philippines. Shortly after arriving in the Philippines they were merged with the 2nd AAF Intelligence Detachment as the war was moving into its final phase and not as many personnel were required.

Hence the photos presented here are a mixed bag. Many photos were taken from fixed mounted cameras at the rear of the aircraft which would be triggered as the plane flew over the target. On other occasions if a photographer was on board, shots would be taken by a hand held camera or 16mm movie camera. Even on a recon mission however, every crewman was vital to the survival of the plane and as such they were usually trained to man a gunner's position as well.

Also regarding images from these collections - while photographers like my uncle actively flew combat and/or recon missions they would also make duplicates of anything passing through the lab that they found interesting or significant.

To confuse matters further, specific mission reports and citation reports from the period and testimonials by surviving photo lab personnel document the fact that some of the staff such as my uncle would fly combat missions at any opportunity. Another Photo Lab veteran - Dick Wiederwax - even managed to get credited with "one kill and two probables". Sometimes these would be volunteer missions assembled at the last minute, other times they might fill a vacancy on an existing mission. For example one last minute volunteer mission John flew on May 8th 1944 to gather recon data on Biak was flown with two B-25D's with pilots from both the 71st Reconnaissance Group and the 8th Photo Reconnaissance Squadron with crews hastily thrown together. Other missions saw John joining up with 22nd, 345th and 90th Bomber Group crews and likely with other groups as well.

Thus many of these images are taken from actions of local Bomber Groups - the 345th, 312th, 38th, 90th, 17th Recon Sqd, as well as personal photos from John Stava and the men themselves. Wherever possible I have credited the origin of the photograph, but accurate determination in some cases is a matter of judgment and in many cases somewhat impossible to be confirmed at this late date.

In the course of researching this book some of the veterans or their families contributed photos which dovetailed with my uncle's service and have been included. So about 80 percent of the images are from my uncle's collection, the balance from other sources which are credited

It should also be noted that source information is occasionally open to dispute - some veteran's interviewed adamantly contradicted certain information given by other veteran's and some written accounts clash with others. I welcome anyone with additional information on these images to contact me directly.

In memory of: John H. Stava 1912-1985

John Henry Stava was born on June 15, 1912 in Oil City, Pennsylvania to John Stava senior, a tailor, and his wife Johanna, both emigrants from Bratislava in what is now Slovakia. He was the third of four children; Robert (my grandfather), Bill, and a younger sister, Josephine. In 1924 the family moved to Cleveland, Ohio. In 1930 John senior was killed walking home from work one night by a car driven by college student.

Prior to the war he worked as a salesman in commercial equipment and supplies. In October of 1940, he enlisted in the Army Air Corps and was sent to Lowry AFB, Colorado, where he trained in aerial photography. Prior to departing overseas he was sent to Laredo AFB, Texas for additional training in aerial gunnery.

In the spring of 1943 he was personally selected by Colonel David W. Hutchison to help establish and put in to operation the 5th AF Advanced Echelon Photo Section, a photo laboratory attached directly to 5th Air Force Advanced Echelon Headquarters under General Ennis C. Whitehead, then based in Port Moresby, New Guinea. In addition to being in charge of the lab which processed photographs 24 hours day, often under the high pressure of combat requirements, John would also frequently volunteer as a photographer/gunner on various combat recon missions, usually on whatever B24's or B25's were available. According to citation reports he officially began flying combat and reconnaissance missions as of September 26th, 1943 and flew in many of the major campaigns of the South Pacific including New Guinea, Bismarck Archipelago, Northern Solomon's, China, Southern Philippines, Luzon, Central Pacific and Air Offensive Japan.

No satisfied to being assigned sporadic recon missions John managed to get transferred to combat status as a tail gunner in the fall of 1944 as the 5th Air Force moved into the Philippines. Records show he was officially assigned to the 17th Recon Squadron but according to the 17th veterans he served with he "wasn't a permanent member" and the evidence indicates he was flying missions with other bomber groups as well, probably being farmed out due to his combined photography/gunner abilities and likely leveraging his connections with 5th A.F. H.Q.. His citation reports appear to validate this - they state that he was flying "Sustained operational flight missions from 22 January 1945 to 10 May 1945, during which hostile contact was probable and expected. These operations consisted of long range photographic reconnaissance missions against enemy airdromes, shipping, and ground installations, during which photographs were taken which furnished valuable intelligence information". Mission reports from the 17th Recon list him strictly as a tail gunner, which would suggest his photographic endeavors occurred elsewhere. Veteran's of the Photo Section commented that he seemed much happier in this new role and would still visit them from time to time. He worked in this capacity until June of 1945, when he was mustered out.

In the course of his service he was awarded a total of 6 bronze stars, the Air Medal with 4 Oak Leaf Clusters, was recommended for the Distinguished Flying Cross, and took hundreds of photographs and film footage. In the summer of 1944 he was recommended by his commanding officers for promotion to Lieutenant, but it never materialized.

Somewhere in his training he achieved pilot certification. His sister Josephine recalled an event shortly after returning from the war where took her up for a flight at the Cleveland Airport in a two-seater trainer and proceeded to fly through a half-hour of acrobatic rolls, loops and dives. It was the first, and after that, last time she would ever set foot in an airplane again.

After the war he settled in Denver, Colorado where he served with the Civil Air Patrol out of Lowry Air Force Base until late 1953.

He died in a Miami Veterans hospital of congestive heart failure on September 13th, 1985.

Off To War

By 1940 War was in full swing in Europe and men like my uncle no doubt saw the writing on the wall and decided to get a head start on things by enlisting. All of his aerial photography training was done at the Photography School at Lowry field in Denver, Colorado, as was most of the Photo Section. Most of their training was confined to the Colorado/Rockies area though some of the prints show they ventured over to the Grand Canyon, Utah and Alaska as well. After photography school John was then sent to Laredo Army Air Field for additional training as an aerial gunner. Many veteran's made it clear that every crew man was vital to the survival of the ship, so even photographers would need to double as gunners if need be.

Most of the photographers in the photo lab were professional photographers in civilian life. Others, like Jack Heyn of the 3rd BG, were simply caught up in the wave of war and found themselves as photographers in the field with no formal training. In Jacks case, he never made it to Lowry due to Pearl Harbor and found himself in Brisbane as one of the Group photographers, learning as he went. Talk about "on the job" training.

Shown here is a small sampling of the collection of photos covering his prewar training, mostly aerial recon shots of the area around Colorado, the Rockies, Alaska, and a few dozen photos covering the graduation day proceedings at Laredo. Outside of my uncle though none of the people in these photos have been identified. Laredo Army Airfield (Later renamed "Laredo Air Force Base") closed permanently in 1973 and today only traces of it still exist - most of the airfield was incorporated into the municipal airport.

(Above) Graduation Day parade at Laredo AF in Texas. Note the early model B-25 in the background. Laredo was one of the better known training schools for gunnery during the war. (John Stava Collection)

(Above) Graduation Day at Laredo AFB in Texas. John Stava, sporting "spats" and an early "doughboy" style helmet in hand, is to the left. (John Stava Collection)

(Left) Play Ball! An anachronism by today's health conscience standards - nothing like smoking a cigarette while playing sports! (John Stava Collection)

(Below) Picnic with the girls. Lucky Strikes, fried chicken and Coca-Cola. This photo was taken at March Field, where the enlisted pool drew plenty of girls. According to Carl Camp: "We called them 'Pool Flies' - they were the dependents of the Senior NCO's who lived on the post - only good for flirting with since they were very much too young or too well guarded for anything else". (John Stava Collection)

(Above) A postcard shot of a Beechcraft AT-7 over Mount McKinley, Alaska, probably on a photo-recon training run. (John Stava Collection)

(Below) Already obsolete - A Douglas B-18 Bomber on another training mission near the Grand Canyon. Vic Tatelman of the 345th Bomber Group had this recollection of basic training: 'Of course flying accidents occurred. For me, it happened in primary: The engine quit on take-off; that sudden silence at 100-feet with airspeed hovering not much over stall; it gets your attention immediately. Basic training and intuition take over instantly - land straight ahead. I did, in an orange grove, between two rows of trees, took off both wings, but I was unhurt. I still have, after 65 years, a piece of the rudder fabric from that PT-22 trainer.' (John Stava Collection)

(Right) John Stava's gunnery diploma from Laredo. Within three months he would be sweating it out in the jungles of New Guinea, perhaps reflecting that his days at the barren Air Force base in Laredo were looking more and more like paradise by comparison. (John Stava Collection)

United States Army

Army Air Forces

Be it known that

TECHNICAL SERGEANT JOHN HENRY STAVA

has satisfactorily completed the course of instruction

prescribed for

AERIAL GUNNERS

at the LAREDO ARMY AIR FIELD *School.*

In testimony whereof and by virtue of vested authority

I do confer upon him this

DIPLOMA

Given at LAREDO, TEXAS *this* twenty-third *day*

of January *in the year of our Lord one thousand*

nine hundred and forty three

William L. Kennedy

WILLIAM L. KENNEDY
COLONEL, AIR CORPS
COMMANDANT

Attest

Louis H. Haring

LOUIS H. HARING
1st Lt., AIR CORPS
SECRETARY

U. S. GOVERNMENT PRINTING OFFICE : 1942—O-446650

New Guinea 1943-44

Rabaul, Vunakanau, Wewak, Buna, Dobodura, Biak, Hollandia, Nadzab, Lae, Kavieng, Port Moresby. Exotic names of exotic sounding places but rattle them off to the average American and I can pretty much guarantee you will be met with a vacant stare. Mention "New Guinea" and you'll probably fare better, perhaps a nod of recognition likely gleaned from a National Geographic or television documentary about an island in the Pacific that calls to mind primitive people running around and where it seems the women haven't discovered shirts yet.

And yet soldiers died there in the tens of thousands. It was the location of some of the most intense fighting in the Pacific and by August of 1942 the Japanese forces had closed within 20 miles* of the sole remaining stronghold, Port Moresby, leaving New Guinea (And pretty much the entire South Pacific for that matter) one city away from being completely taken over by the Japanese, which would have put them practically within waving distance of Australia. Although apparently the Japanese had no plans to actually invade Australia, they would be able to effectively isolate them from the West and have complete control of the Pacific.

It was that close a call.

Few people are aware that New Guinea is the second largest island on this planet, twice the size of Japan and over 1300 miles long. If you laid it over the United States and put one end in New York City the other end would be in Omaha Nebraska.

Capt. Donald Hough and Capt Elliott Arnold in their book "Big Distance" had this rather colorful description of the campaign in New Guinea:

"Fighting with airplanes in the Southwest Pacific was an anachronism greater than that of the Yankee who invaded King Arthur's court with a firearm. It would have been closer in time and understanding and relative civilizations if suddenly we had found ourselves fighting over medieval Europe or in the French and Indian wars or with Cortez and the Aztecs.

"The Pacific to us was ancient beyond understanding."

(Above) Standard issue "Tour Guide" given to American Soldiers arriving in New Guinea.

Looking at a map of New Guinea and the Southwest Pacific hardly conveys the exotic flavor and sheer distances of the campaign there. Missions that took our airmen 7 - 8 hours, sometimes over vast stretches of empty ocean were not uncommon. But it's safe to say it was the one of the pivotal battlegrounds of the Pacific. It was where in 1942 a no-nonsense stocky little man named General George Kenney would be brought in by General MacArthur to rebuild the shattered remnants of the Far Eastern Air Forces there into a cohesive fighting unit, The Fifth Air Force.

The inhospitable nature of the interior of New Guinea dictated that the war would be confined to the coastal regions and as such would be unique from all other theaters of the war. It would be primarily an Air Force driven operation, with the Navy and ground troops playing a supporting role. To succeed Kenney would be forced to improvise and develop new strategies and tactics that focused on destroying then capturing the enemy's airfields and crippling his shipping.

"When we brought airplanes into the sweating jungle islands of the Pacific we stepped back thousands of years"

Capt. Donald Hough and Capt Elliott Arnold, "Big Distance"

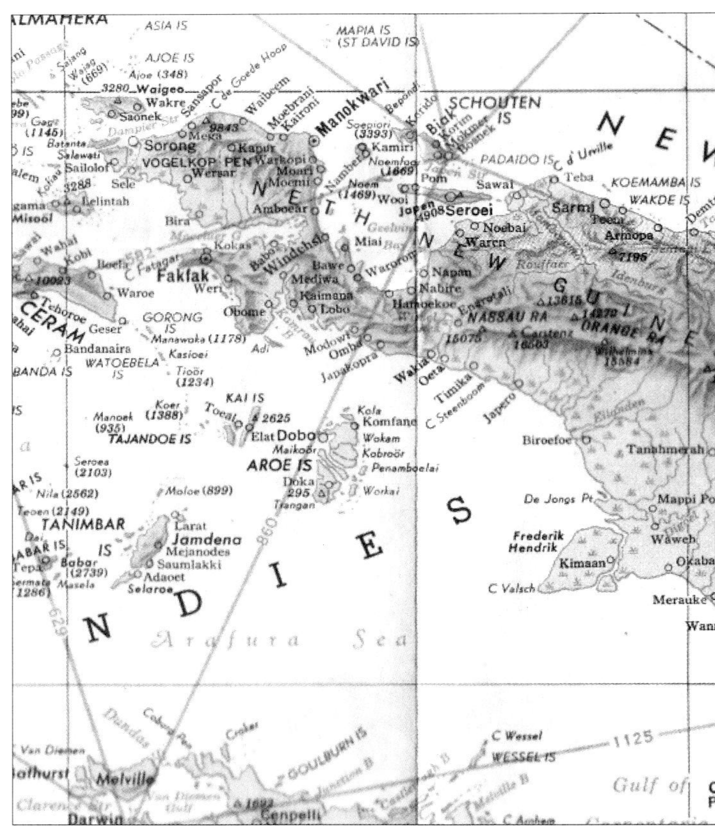

Kenney did that and more yet despite racking up an amazing track record of successes for the next three years the Fifth Air Force would remain the "backwoods cousin" to the war effort in Europe, left to make do with whatever leftover's the powers in Washington would toss their way.

By the time the 5th A.F. Photo Lab showed up in Port Moresby in May of 1943 the war in the Pacific was clearly in the Allies favor. Buna on the opposite side of the Owen Stanley Mountains had been retaken the previous November, March had seen the Allies give the Japanese a bloody nose in the Battle of the Bismarck Sea and pressure was being brought to bear on Japanese bases further up the Northeast Coast at Salamaua, Lae, and Madang. Late summer would see a series of raids to smash

* *Accounts vary on this - 30 miles is often quoted, some say as close as 12 miles.*

the Japanese Army Air bases around the Wewak area, September would see the innovative paratroop invasion of Nadzab, and October and November would see a series of devastating attacks on Rabaul - the "Gibraltar of the Pacific", effectively neutralizing it as a base. In December the Western part of New Britain would be invaded and the Allied Forces would continue leapfrogging up the Northern Coast, by-passing and isolating large pockets of Japanese soldiers, leaving them to "wither on the vine" In the Wewak area alone, nearly thirty thousand Japanese soldiers would be cut off, left to die of starvation and disease, abandoned by their army. The situation would become terrible for the beleaguered Japanese 18th army and when they finally surrendered in September of 1945 their commander Lt. General Hataso had to be physically carried out on a chair to sign the papers.

The New Guinea campaign would wrap up in July and August of 1944 with the occupation of Biak, a stark island bristling with caves that the Japanese would defend to the death. From there the Allies would be poised to retake the Philippines.

(Above) A Liberty ship easing into Port Moresby. (John Stava Collection)

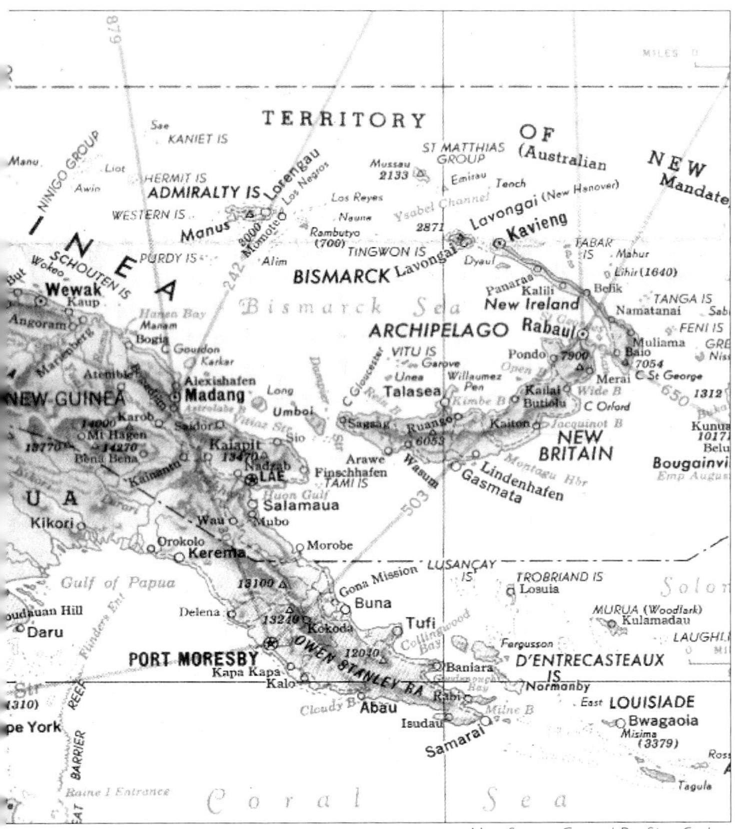

Map Source: General Drafting Co. Inc.

Life in New Guinea was quite an adjustment for the American servicemen. Setting aside a tenacious and merciless enemy, they would have to confront unimaginatable weather conditions and the harsh realities of jungle living.

Heat and intense humidity were a daily condition. Our men had to deal with assorted body fungi, multiple varieties of malaria, dengue fever, and a host of bugs and parasites Many would be afflicted by these things for the rest of their natural lives. Food was less than terrible and safe drinking water was a premium.

Weather, particularly in the early days of the campaign when faced with crossing the Owen Stanley Mountains daily, was just as dangerous as the enemy. Raging storm fronts over the mountains were the norm, and often flights - laden with bombs - would have to navigate the fronts and find "tunnels" in the storm systems to get through. Violent updrafts and downdrafts would toss the aircraft around like toys, sometimes breaking bones, other times slamming them into the mountain sides. It was not uncommon for aircraft and their crews to disappear on a mission without a trace and over sixty years later there are still more than ninety planes and crews unaccounted for. 38th BG pilot Garrett Middlebrook put it this way: "If the FAA today caught us at what we were doing then - flying bomb laden aircraft through violent thunderstorms with no navigational beacons and only the crudest navigation aides, then to fly into an enemy target, skipping bombs into ships at masthead height, then flying back through the storms again...they'd of had us locked up and put in straightjackets."

All that, and yes you still had to go fight the enemy.

The Japanese were a tenacious and often merciless foe. The military culture that controlled the country at the time was vastly different from ours in that it was fanatically harsh and unforgiving - soldiers were trained to fight to the death and the concept of surrender was considered shameful and unacceptable. They were equally harsh to their own soldiers as to their enemy and as such their treatment of prisoners was brutal compared to the Allies. It was well known by allied airmen that unless you were an officer the odds were you would be executed if captured, usually by the sword.

At the time the Japanese for the most part despised us as much as we them, each side considering the other to be an inferior race with inferior soldiers. Certainly this cultural and ethnic gap made it all the easier to demonize the enemy and rationalize the killing that had to be done, a dilemma not so easily achieved in the European Theater.

In New Guinea it seemed as if inertia seized the Japanese high command after their initial victories in the SW Pacific, as if the aggressive Allied response and refusal to cave in confounded them. This was due in part to a non-unified command structure in the theater, a lack of cooperation between Japanese Army and Navy units as well as air and ground units, a refusal to break with outdated military protocols and an almost criminal negligence of the needs of soldiers fighting in such a hostile environment.

Regardless, in spite of being vastly out numbered in men and aircraft, General Kenney and his underdog 5th Air Force quickly turned the fortunes of war against the Japanese by sheer guts, ingenuity, and improvising tactics on the fly.

5th Air Force Photo Lab

Also referred to as the 5th AF Advanced Echelon Photo Section and a variety of other titles, they were a unit of about 18 men that was formed in early 1943 to handle photography processing directly for 5th AF Headquarters. The unit was assembled by Colonel David W. Hutchison at the 5th A.F. Base in Pittsburg, California and was initially brought over to Brisbane where they trained briefly with the Australians at Archerfield Airdrome. In April/May of 1943 they would move up to Port Moresby in New Guinea where the lab would be officially put into operation with the Fifth Air Force Advanced Echelon (or Advon), which was General Kenney's forward operations command. John Stava would accompany bomber crews as photographer and/or gunner on the key raids against Rabaul in October and November of 1943. By the summer of 1944 they would move up to Nadzab with the rest of 5th AF Advon and from there to Owi, Mindaro, then Luzon, by which time they would merge with the 2nd AAF Intelligence Section.

The lab was under the command of General Ennis Whitehead. Below him was Colonel Hutchison, then Major L. A. Tockstien, Captain Pen L. Gooldy (Jr) and Captain Gingerich. They operated twenty-four hours a day in two shifts, "often under the high pressure of combat requirements" and working in a sweltering photo lab in the jungles of New Guinea was hardly a picnic. As 3rd Bomber Group photographer Jack Heyn pointed out: *"Processing film in New Guinea in the '40s was a challenge. Recommended temperature for solutions is 68 degrees. Day time temps were always over 100 and our solutions were seldom under 90 degrees. If you ran film thru that the emulsion would flow off the backing. So you ran the film thru an alum bath to harden the emulsion then into the developer."* Somehow they made it work - after 60 years the photos are still holding up fine.

One of the difficulties in researching this book is that there are no remaining official records of the labs existence - only interviews with the few surviving members and these photos provided any information of who they were and what they did.

(Below) *A somewhat crudely made montage of the photo lab in action. The center picture shows the photo lab building in Nadzab, with John Stava at his desk lower left and Captain Penn L. Gooldy lower right. Described as easygoing, Captain Gooldy was a very popular commander with the team.* (John Stava Collection)

(Above) *John Stava takes five and has a smoke - one of the fringe benefits of being in the lab is they regularly got plenty of free cigars and cigarettes.* (John Stava Collection)

(Above Right) *Fred Miller of Montana heads off to the showers. All (drinking) water had to be heavily treated with chemicals and then placed in rubber "Lyster" bags.* (John Stava Collection)

(Right) *"Off to Chow" - Dick Wiederwax, Bob Crowe and William E. A. Johnstone with mess kits. Bob Crowe was an invaluable source of information regarding the Photo Lab's functions and personnel. The poor quality of the food in New Guinea was notorious, which may explain the glum expressions.* (John Stava Collection)

(Below Left & Right) *Paul Kaase of Galveston, Texas transcribing notes at Dick Widerwax's desk. The "dame" on the wall in the background is the same photo lower right, which was important enough to make it back to the states. On the back of the photo was written: "To Dick: The first person I've ever met! I'll wait for you., Dear, Patricia." Dicks' son Marc, who sent me her photo, added "P.S. - this is not my MOM."* (Left photo: John Stava Collection, Right Photo courtesy of Marc Wiederwax)

(Above) *Jim "Mac" MacKeever guards the photo supplies.* (John Stava Collection)

(Above right) *Look important -Capt. Gooldy, Major Tockstein and Capt Gingerich at operations in a staged looking shot.* (John Stava Collection)

(Opposite page upper left) *Bill Johnstone and Jim MacKeever examine a roll of 9" Negative which likely would have come from the fixed mounted camera on the back of a B25 or A20. Jack Heyn, a 3rd BG Photographer explained the camera situation as thus: "We had 4 aerial cameras that were used on missions. The K-17 and K-18 used a 9 inch roll of film 150 ft. long. The 17 gave a 9"x9" negative, 18 gave a 9"x18" negative. The other two used a 5 inch roll of film. I believe it was the K-20 that was also a mounted camera and gave a 5"x7" negative, the other was a hand held camera that gave a 4"x5" negative - don't remember its designation. It was usually carried by a gunner." (Author: The K20 was the 4x5 "Handheld camera", all were made by Fairchild Camera Co. in Queens, New York).* (John Stava Collection)

(Opposite page upper right) *Sgt. Walter "Doc" Kaszubowski from Chicago at the enlarger. Apparently not the most popular guy in the lab from the beginning., on the first day they started working in Brisbane Captain Gooldy showed up and gave everyone a lecture "You guys have got to stop telling Sgt. Kaz to "Blow it out his ass"!"* (John Stava Collection)

(Opposite page lower Right) *It's not that often you find a photo of your uncle having a drink with a General, let alone the one in charge of the 5th Air Force!. This very unusual photo taken at the "3rd Slug Bar" Dobodura in September of 1943 when General Kenney was visiting the base courtesy of the 3rd BG commander "Jock" Henebry (see page 38). It was originally posted on Peter Dunne's outstanding "Oz at War" website by Jack Heyn with the caption "Outside of General Kenney and myself, can't I.D. any of these guys" I got a hold of Jack and told him "Hell I can - they're the guys from the 5th AF Photo Lab!" From left to right: Richard Wiederwax, John Stava, Paul Kaase, Captain Gooldy, General Kenny, Jack Heyn, Walter 'Doc' Kaszubowski" What's unusual is that most of these men are Sergeants and the "Slug Bar" was an officers only club. At the time some of the lab were flying along missions to Rabaul doubling as gunner/photographers, Author Lex McAuley's take was "As Kenney was el Supremo I guess he could invite the sergeants into the Officers' Club and put the drinks on his tab".* (Photo courtesy of Jack Heyn)

(Below right) *Joe Wydra from Cleveland, Ohio. One of the original crew from the states, he had a reputation as "quite an exaggerator" He passed away in the 1950's* (John Stava Collection)

(Below left) *Fred Miller kills some time with a dime store novel. Fred was another invaluable source of information on the photo lab.* (John Stava Collection)

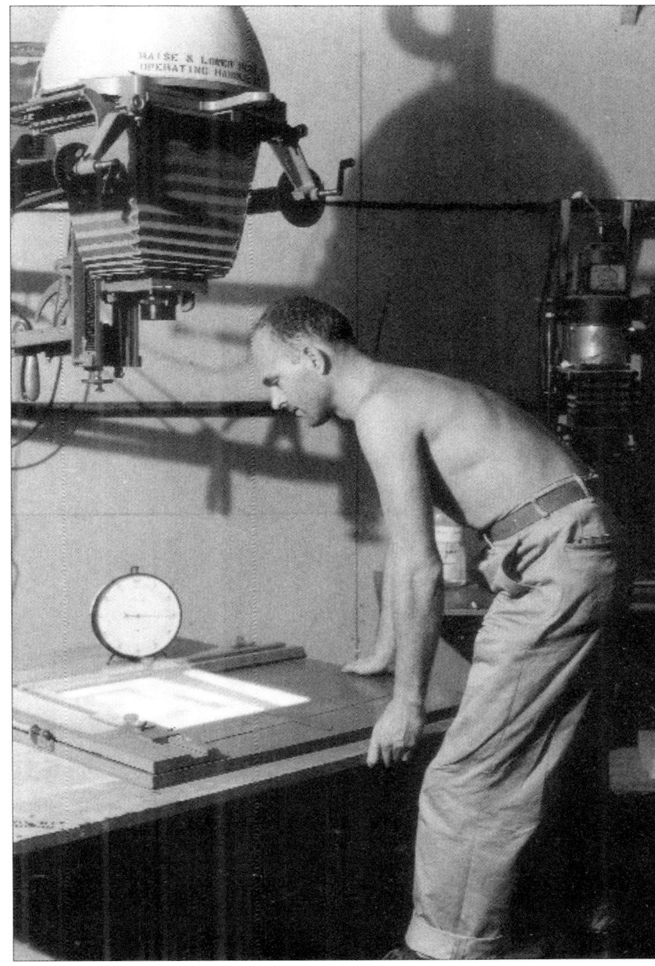

(Above) The 5th AF Photo lab team doing some exploring, around what appears to be a front landing gear of a P-38. Richard Wiederwax, center, is holding a .50 cal ammo belt - a souvenir? Alvin "Whitey" White is on the right. Fred Miller had read somewhere that massaging the scalp could grow your hair back, so he gave Alvin a scalp massage every morning and claimed he grew back some "fuzz". Wiederwax was quite a character, always getting himself assigned to some interesting job or another. He later transferred to an air/sea rescue unit flying in PBY Catalinas. (Photo courtesy of Marc Wiederwax)

(Above right) Bill Johnstone from Alabama poses on an outcropping in the foothills outside of Port Moreseby. Bill served as the clerk for the Photo Lab. (John Stava Collection)

(Below) From the same series as above, Jim MacKeever and Richard Wiederwax looking like a couple of rough customers. The hydraulics tank attached to the landing gear in the background appears to be riddled with bullet holes. (Photo courtesy of Marc Wiederwax)

John Stava Collection

(Above) John Stava at his desk at Nadzab. This photo was taken around late July/August of 1944 - the photo just over his shoulder was from a famous 312th BG mission to Ceram on July 15th. (See page 54 for a full size of this image). Fred Miller described John as an "Unusual person. Very, very calm. He always had a look like he was daydreaming, but he wasn't daydreaming at all. He was neither a good-looking or bad-looking guy, lean, thin, with blondish brown hair and blue eyes. He had a dry sense of humor - he had a way of telling a story and making it twice as funny" (John Stava Collection)

(Below left) A sample of the K-17c 12 inch Aerial Camera manufactured by the Fairchild Camera Company in Queens, N.Y. Not exactly your Kodak instamatic. (Image courtesy of www.AerialPhotoLab.com)

(Below right) A rare shot of a B-24 waist gunner in combat taken by Jerome Schrenk of the 22nd BG. John often doubled as a gunner on his missions. (Jerome Schrenk Collection)

Local Flavor: New Guinea

For the average American in the 1940's the New Guinea natives must have been something of a culture shock. Called "Fuzzy Wuzzies" by the servicemen, relations generally proved to by amicable - depending on the local chieftan's alliances. Of course there was still the rare unfortunate incident of worse things, such as three members of Lt. Hank Chovanec's 90th BG crew surviving a crash landing in the mountains near the village of Bena Bena fifty miles inland of Mandang in April of 1943 only to be killed and devoured by their rescuers, but by the 1940's cannibal tribes by and large remained only in remote mountain areas.

Australian Royal Navy veteran Kenny King recalled local New Guinea men that would squat on their haunches a deliver the "Damndest most ear splitting howl that would make your hair stand up on end". Although not apparent in these black and white images, native men often chewed betel nuts and rubbed the juice through their hair, giving their teeth and heads a bright red sheen Jack Heyn recalled: *"During the Kokoda, Buna/Gona, Sananandа Point campaigns the natives were 'Black Angels'. They literally carried a lot of the wounded out of those jungles. They were helpful in a lot of ways, we even had a laundry boy at one point. But I'll tell you, for 22 months the only white females we saw were the gals with Gary Cooper, Bob Hope and Judith Anderson's USO troops."* Jack should have hooked up with Dick Wiederwax, who had an uncanny ability for finding women where no-one else could, even in Port Moresby.

Since the 1940's New Guinea has come a long way towards modernization and except for the deep inland regions the primitive dress and lifestyle in these images are all but gone.

(Below left) A photo straight out of "National Geographic" - a local outing led by New Guinea guides near Nadzab. Other photos in this series show that a couple Australians were along for the ride, although the exact purpose of this trip is unknown. Just sight-seeing perhaps, but in this photo there's a suspiciously square crate under the water to the right.... (John Stava Collection)

(Below right) The "Hey, what the hell?" look on this New Guinea woman's face paints a portrait of a shrewd and slightly suspicious customer. (John Stava Collection)

(Opposite page) Nice shot of young New Guinea boys scaling coconut trees. Falling "missiles" were an occupational hazard in the area, although a great source of nutritious meat and milk. The soldiers' "Pocket Guide to New Guinea" refers to coconut juice as the "Pop" of the Tropics, though cautions over consumption for "digestive" reasons. I think we can figure out what that means. Note this picture is also on the wall behind John's desk on page 15. (John Stava Collection)

(This page top and bottom) Various photos of Hanuabado Village near Port Moresby, which was a scene of much bargaining with the servicemen. Boats, grass skirts, combs and necklaces were made here by the natives when not doing some kind of work for the ANGAU (Australian New Guinea Administrative Unit). The dog in the photo upper right adds a nice domestic touch to the scene, although in some areas I understand they sometimes they wound up on the dinner plate. Kenny King recalled several natives he met wearing necklaces of dog's teeth. In General Kenney's words: "The huts looked picturesque, kept out the rain, afforded shelter from the sun, and were nice things to stand in front of while you had your picture taken to send home to your folks, but after a short time they served as homes for a million varieties of spiders, scorpions, centipedes, lizards, and even birds. Luckily they were highly flammable and accordingly, through accident or design, you didn't stay in the same house too long." A hybrid language called "Pidgin English" was used for communication in many instances. Some of the terminology was pretty colorful, such as "man ee go-go-go-go-go" for "It's pretty far" or "Grass belong head" for "hair" Personally I like "Short fella trousers" for "Shorts". (John Stava Collection)

(Opposite Top) Hanging out with the band. A Red Cross nurse flashes a tight smile in an almost but not quite cutting it "having-a-great-time" Kodak moment. She appears in a few different photos, always looking a little out of her element. (John Stava Collection)

(Opposite middle left) Postcard shot of a young native woman posing on the beach. (John Stava Collection)

(Opposite middle right) Band on the run - looks like a photo op as the boys head down the road, possibly to another gig. (John Stava Collection)

(Opposite bottom) Another posed shot at Hanuabado village, nurses with the native children. Looks like there was no shortage of bananas. New Guinea fruit were generally safe to eat provided the skin was unbroken. However, New Guinea proved to be a cornocupia of diseases for our servicemen - cholera, malaria, dysentery, typhoid fever, Dengue fever, encephalitis, hepatitis B, Tuberculosis, filariasis, just to name a few - and it was advised to avoid any direct physical contact with natives. Although I've never heard of any accounts of sexual relations between servicemen and native women, certainly the government boys thought it a possibility - the handy pocket guide mentions that "Gonorrhea is very common, so is a venereal disease known as yaws, which resembles syphilis but is milder. Whether it's mild or not, you can't be too careful! If you have sexual contact, by all means take a prophylaxis as promptly as possible. The importance of this cannot be overstressed....not only to you now but to you and yours when you get home." (John Stava Collection)

(Clockwise from upper left) 1) Unknown street scene, possibly in Lae, with Australian soldiers 2). Deep in the Kunai Grass with Australian soldiers. Kunai grass, the bane of many an airmen who went down in the jungle, could grow up to 12 feet high. It made for hard going and was sharp enough to cut skin. 3) Native canoe outside of Port Moresby. The shark emblem on the sail was another grim reminder for airmen that ditched at sea 4) Another scenic landscape shot of New Guinea. (John Stava Collection)

(Opposite Page) A magnificent shot of waterfalls somewhere in the foothills outside of Port Moresby. Despite the daily grind of war, it's interesting that some photographers like John still found time to pause and document the primordial beauty around them. (John Stava Collection)

1.

2.

"Other than the tropical heat, the mosquitoes, the thick rain-forest/jungle, it was pretty much as suspected."

-Captain Vic Tatelman, 499th BS, 345th BG

4.

3.

(Above Top) *At the 91st Recco Bar John Stava (center) seems to have made some new friends. Second from left Is Stuart Hess, also from the Photo Section. The painting in the background appears to be a creative rendition of New York City. The word "Rockaway" is just visible in the background, either "Far Rockaway or Rockaway Beach", either place still worth a visit in Brooklyn.* (John Stava Collection)

(Above Left) *Looks like this party starting to go to pieces.* (John Stava Collection)

(Above Right) *"Doc" Kaszubowski takes a turn on the dance floor. It's not clear who these women are, most likely nurses from the local field hospital, but the same ones appear in numerous photos, no doubt a pleasant sight for women starved eyes.* (John Stava Collection)

(Top left and right) More photos from the 91st Recco bar. In the top left photo are some key personnel from the Photo Lab. From L-R : Unknown, Paul Kaas and Stuart "Bud" Hess with friend. Stuart A. Hess, from Florida, was described thus: "Nothing slowed him down, give him anything to repair and he'd go at it.". On the right the "Recco's" band swings into a nother number beneath a jury-rigged parachute ceiling. The "91st Reccos" refers to the 91st Tactical Reconnaissance Wing, under which was the 71st Tactical Recon Group and the 6th Photographic Group, which consisted of 4 squadrons including the 20th Mapping BS (See aircraft on page 94) and the 8th Photo Reconnaissance SQ. (Also called the "Eightballers"). The "EightBall" newsletter of December 12th 1943 notes that "The new 9 o'clock closing of Club Bars on this fair island have met with so-so approval" and that the Club Committee revealed that "Sales hadn't dropped much. The men feel much better the next day." (John Stava Collection)

(Bottom) These four photos show festivities at the the "Advon EM (Enlisted Men's) Club which catered to all the non-officers in General Whitehead's Advanced Echelon staff. Entertainment in New Guinea was a commodity there were no fixed establishments or towns (In the western sense) for off duty soldiers to carouse in. Each group therefore had to scratch build their own "clubs". I haven't unearthed any further details about this particular clubs existence, but the guys at the bar look pretty happy to be there. (John Stava Collection)

U.S.O. Shows

U.S.O. Shows were staple entertainment for the servicemen during WWII, and with his 5th Air Force photographer credentials John had ample opportunity to photograph many of their stars in candid moments. He was able to cover one rare show in the states with both Bob Hope and Jack Benny and their troupes on the same bill - this would have been prior to his shipping out to New Guinea. Later on he would have a rare opportunity to photograph Jack Benny & Co. again at Nadzab during August of 1944.

(Above) *Never a shy one, Bob Hope jumps in and rubs elbows with his audience - John wrote on the back of the picture: "These guys are all laughing at me because I was laughing so damned hard at Hope. I could hardly take the picture. The more I laughed -the more he mugged--which made me laugh all the harder" This photo was taken at a USO show in the gymnasium at March Field in California, in early 1942. Carl Camp, a gunner from the 90th Bomb Group whom John would fly with on a mission two years later (see page 67) was also at this show. It's proximity to Los Angeles and Hollywood made it a convenient stop for movie stars, singers, comedians and popular bands. Note the lack of unit insignia on many of the soldiers here indicates they are trainees and the shoulder patch on the corporal to the right was generally phased out in late 1941.* (John Stava Collection)

(Far Left) *Jerry Colonna with his high reedy voice takes center stage, while Skinnay Ennis handles conductor duties.* (John Stava Collection)

(Near Left) *Showgirls from Sydney strike a pose at one of the "theater's" at Port Moresby. One veteran interviewed commented wryly: "Yeah, they entertained in a couple different ways.". On the back John had scrawled "I like the blonde - front and center!"* (John Stava Collection)

(Above) *Jack Benny mugs it up with a very fetching Carole Landis during the New Guinea U.S.O. tour in mid-August of 1944, at Nadzab The two officers in front haven't been identified but in the back row from left to right are: Larry Adler, June Bruner, Jack Benny, Carole Landis, Martha Tilton. Sadly, four years later Carole would take her own life - despondent over a failed affair with actor Rex Harrison who wouldn't leave his wife. Her health never fully recovered from this USO tour. Larry Adler was a fast talking Jewish kid from Baltimore who became a virtuoso harmonica player and singer who made a name for himself in Benny's show. Martha Tilton was also a regular on Benny's show.* (John Stava Collection)

(Right) *God knows what Harpo Marx is up to in this photo, but singer Judith Anderson seems to be taking it in stride.* (John Stava Collection)

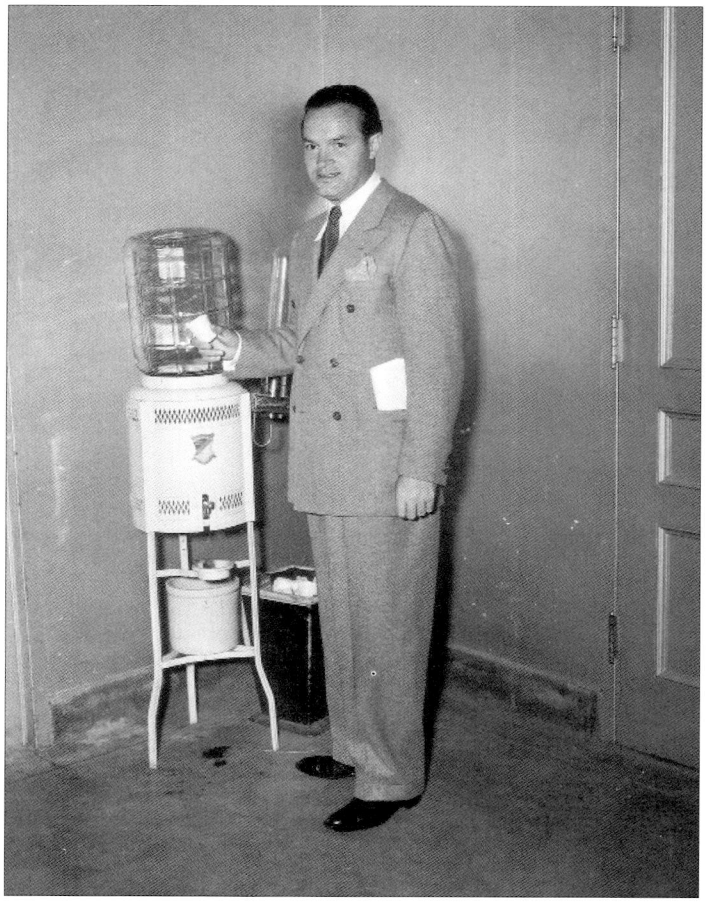

(Top left) *Caught red-handed! Bob Hope sneaks a cup by the water cooler at the same USO show at March field in 1942. None of the wartime buildings that were there exist to today.* (John Stava Collection)

(Top right) *Jive Dancing. Eddie "Rochester" Anderson was a staple sidekick in Jack Benny's routine. Starting out with what was supposed to be a one show deal in 1936, the chemistry and wit between the two was such that they wound up performing together for another 20 years. Anderson appeared in numerous films including "Gone With The Wind". Hardly a sidekick relationship with Benny, Anderson gave as good as he got.* (John Stava Collection)

(Bottom left) *Par for the course. Crooner Bing Crosby is joined by friends for a few swings at a celebrity open in California.* (John Stava Collection)

(Bottom right) *Jack Benny takes the stage. One of his trademark routines was about a night he gets help up by a guy with a gun. 'You're money or your life' the thug asks. After a long pause he asks again "What's it going to be, your money or your life?" to which Benny replies impatiently "I'm thinking, I'm thinking...."* (John Stava Collection)

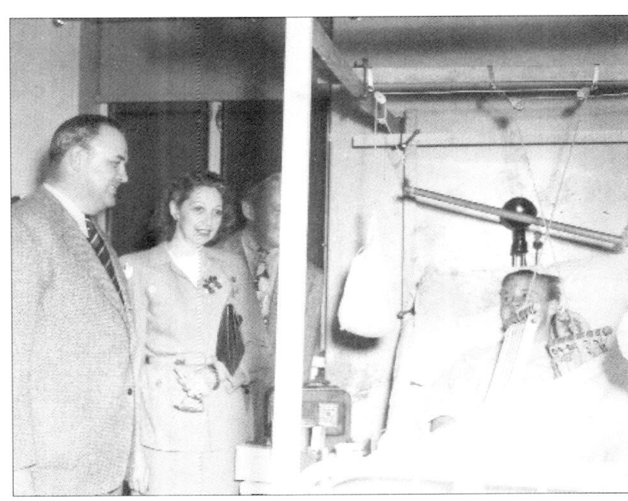

(Top) *General Whitehead mugs it up with actor Gary Cooper (kneeling) who came through New Guinea in 1943. The blonde appears to have the hots for the general - she appears in a few photos with the same rapt expression.* (Robert Stava Collection)

(Bottom left) *The outdoor stage at Port Moresby, same as in the Sydney Showgirls" photo on page 24. The movie playlist of December 1943 notes "Five Graves to Cairo and "Above Suspicion" were playing at the time. Kenny King recounted in a rather colorful tale that the Japanese had gotten so close to Port Moreseby that they would sneak into the theater at night when movies were playing at which point soldiers were advised to carry sidearms and flashlights. He claimed that every so often you would hear a "Hey Joe, got a cigarette?" followed by a flashlight click and a blam! Possibly I was getting my leg pulled but an amusing story nonetheless.* (Photo couortesy Marc Wiederwax)

(Bottom right) *Part of the stateside U.S.O. included a trip to the base hospital. Note Jack Benny standing behind the post on the right.* (John Stava Collection)

Northeast Coast 1943

By late July and early August of 1943 the supply system of Japanese barges along the northeast coast of New Guinea was becoming enough of a problem that 5th AF Command started running "barge sweep" missions to wipe them out. Sometimes the job would get up close and personal, as 38th BG Pilot Garrett Middlebrook recounted on this August 2nd sweep: "*When I opened fire I was a few yards long; instead of adjusting I merely held the firing pin down and lowered my nose. My fire power seemed to walk across the water back toward me until it met the barge. Always it was the same. A miniature dust storm exploded with pieces of equipment being torn and scattered in all directions. Although it was not the first time I had witnessed the event, the sight of human bodies being catapulted out of the barge and into the water was a shocking surprise.*"

And as he commented elsewhere in his book, "Air Combat at 20 Feet", once the soldiers on those barges heard the sound of the B-25's their life expectancy went from years to hours down to minutes and seconds.

(Below) *As the Allies air power began to dominate the skies over New Guinea, it became more and more unhealthy for Japanese transports to traverse open waters to supply their beleaguered garrisons along the coast, so they adopted a system of using shallow draft camouflaged barges that would sneak along the coast by night and "hide" during the day. The ruse doesn't seem to be working if the intention of this 500lb bomb dropped by 38th Bomber Group B-25's over Borgen Bay, New Britain on July 29th , 1943 is any indication.* (John Stava Collection)

(Opposite page above) *On July 28th B-25 strafers caught up with this Japanese destroyer also at Borgen Bay, hitting her 14 times and finally finishing her off the next day.* (John Stava Collection)

(Opposite Bottom) More barges run out of luck in this shot taken at at Raun Bay, November 9th, 1943. Typically they would hug hide along the coastlines during the daylight hours and only travel at night for obvious reasons. What these barges were doing out in open water is anyone's guess. (John Stava Collection)

(Above) *Wrong place at the wrong time. A Japanese "Tess" goes down the hard way on August 21st, 1943 after wandering out of the clouds and into the gunsights of 380th BG B24 "Juarez Whistle" flown by Captain Gus Connery. Pulling up alongside the equally startled Japanese pilot he ordered his gunners to open fire and they made short work of the transport. The "Tess" was the Japanese version of the C-47, originally built under license before the war.* (John Stava Collection)

(Opposite page) *A nearly pristine Japanese Nakajima Ki-49 Donryu "Helen" sits parked in a coconut grove at Rapopo Airfield near Rabaul, blissfully unaware that it is moments away from its destruction as parafrag bombs slowly float down. Probably taken on the October 18th, 1943 strike. "Parafrag" bombs, an innovation cooked up by General Kenney himself during the pre-war years, were equally effective against both men and aircraft.. The 24lb bombs had a "feeler" at the end - dropped in clumps they would quietly drift down until contacting a surface, sending deadly shrapnel in all directions. Initially they cost a lot of additional damage to the Japanese - first because they continued to drift down and explode after the bombers had passed overhead, a nasty surprise to unsuspecting onlookers who emerged from cover after the attackers were gone, and second because after a raid many of the unexploded bombs would litter the area, hanging from trees, lying in the grass, hung from the tails of aircraft. Early attempts to remove them safely resulted in a few fatalities, then Japanese soldiers got wise and took to machine-gunning them at a distance to set them off.* (John Stava Collection)

September 1943

After the opening blows to the four airdromes in the Wewak area in August of '43 the Fifth decided to follow up with a second round of attacks on September 27th, 1943, just to let the Japanese there know they hadn't forgotten about them. A combined force of 117 B-24's and B-25's worked over the airfields, accompanied by 129 P-38's and P-40's.

Barely a month previous 38th BG Pilot Garrett Middlebrook had paid several nerve-wracking visits to this area. How did one deal with the fear of flying into combat with the enemy? Every airman dealt with this in his own way, but Garrett's take was *"Any person who pretended (and some did) that he did not feel cold, penetrating fear at such a time was either abnormal or he was an outrageous liar...however, I had come to understand that fear was not the most damaging emotion, terror was. Terror paralyzed my actions but fear did not."*

By the time of these September raids attrition was taking it's toll - as evinced by the amount of derelict aircraft in these photos. Nonetheless 40 aircraft were claimed destroyed on the ground and another 8 in aerial combat.

(Below) *View out the back from a 38th BG B-25 on the bombing run down the Dagua Airfield runway in September of 1943. The Japanese Air Force lacked the heavy engineering equipment that the Allies enjoyed and consequently many of their airdromes in New Guinea tended to be crude by comparison. Additionally they lacked any effective means of dealing with tropical diseases such as Malaria and Dengue fever and their soldiers suffered greatly from these maladies in addition to the mysterious "Wewak fever" which claimed many lives. To make matters worse, once the Fifth began a regular pattern of bombing these airfields the craters would prove to be a perfect breeding ground for these diseases, further exacerbating the problem. Japanese High-Command was unsympathetic to the conditions in the field. On the other hand, the Americans had very regimented procedures for minmizing diseases which included digging trenches to remove standing water, spraying insecticide and even washing clothes in DDT (which would leave your clothes stiff enough to stand on their own).* (Photo courtesy of Marc Wiederwax)

(Opposite Top & Bottom) *Additional shots of the same raid on Dagua with bombs being dropped into the jungle where the Japanese would often place their supply dumps. Despite the excessive loss of aircraft the Japanese Army Airforce continued to funnel planes and men into the area until the spring of 1944 with no apparent strategy other than to throw more fodder into the killing fields. Entire squadrons would be annhilated here in the New Gulnea meatgrinder. Of the 30,000 Japanese troops that wound up cut off here, only 3,000 would survive to surrender at the end of the war, the rest mostly wiped out by starvation and disease. The situation would grow so terrible that some groups of Japanese soldiers would gather on the beaches in huddles to get mowed down by passing Allied strafers, death by enemy fire being a far more honorable way out. There were also reports of cannibalism which were kept from the media at the time.* (Photos courtesy of Marc Wiederwax)

(Opposite Top) *A Ki21 Helen Bomber at Dagua getting shot up. The neatly - and abandoned - bombs lined up on the ground suggest this plane was getting loaded up for a mission.* (Photo courtesy of Marc Wiederwax)

(Opposite Left) *On September 27th, 1943 anti-aircraft postions at Boram get their photo taken by a 5th AF photographic crew and get a few parafrags in return. Note the gunners cringing along the sides of the gun emplacements. Dick Wiederwax flew on this mission as one of the photographers.* (Photo courtesy of Marc Wiederwax)

(Above & Left) *The paratroop assault on Nadzab on September 5th was the largest Allied airborne assault to date. Fortunately it went off like clockwork. 1700 airborne troops along with 36 Australian artillerymen with guns were dropped amid smokescreens and secured the Nadzab area immediately. White parachutes were used for troops and colored ones for supplies and ammuninition. General's MacArthur, Kenney, and Sutherland we're so excited about the drop they insisted on having ringside seats, which were provided by three B17's of the 43rd Bomber Group. The tremendous heat and humidity was so intense many paratroopers collapsed within an hour in the kunai grass, however the Nadzab strip was put in shape within one day and transports started landing reinforcements and supplies immediately. Nadzab would give the 5th Air Force control of the Markham Valley and their first major base of operations on the northern coast. Two weeks later on September 15th, Lae, the coastal base to the southeast, would fall.* (John Stava Collection)

Rabaul 1943

Since it's uneventful capture in January of 1942 - in the aftermath of Pearl Harbor and the fall of the Philippines the city fell in one day with only 16 Japanese casualties - the Japanese had steadily built up their base at Rabaul in New Britain until it had become the "Gibralter of the Pacific". Next to the bases around Wewak it was the largest Japanese base in the SW Pacific area and a thorn in MacArthurs side. The intitial plan to invade it was ultimately set aside as too costly and unnecessary, although western New Britain would be taken in December of 1943 Instead it was decided to neutralize the Japanese forces in a series of consecutive knock out strikes by medium and heavy bombers in October and November of 1943. Rabaul would be isolated and left to wither on the vine, the ragged remains of it's garrison not surrendering formally until early Sepember of 1945.

The photos here are from the October and November raids when Rabaul was at the peak of it's strength. The first, on October 12th was set up as a one-two punch: 113 B-25's of the 3rd, 38th, and 345th Bomber Groups would go in first at low level and and strafe the airfields and AA positions with machine guns and parafrag bombs. The 90th and 43rd Heavy Bomb Groups would follow at around 18,000 feet to finish the job. As author Lex McAulay decribed it: "Against the 50,000 Japanese defenders, fewer than 2,000 Allied airmen were preparing to attack, across merciless seas and jungles, through dangerous flying weather, knowing prisoners rarely survived." The October 12 raid was followed up by subsequent missions, the largest being on October 25th, 29th and November 2nd. Rabaul was the site of another set of tragedies that largely remain unsolved to this day - the fate of thousands of allied prisoners that vanished while under Japanese interment. Many wound up in mass graves outside the city.

(Below) *Sky high view of the the Japanese warships in Simpson harbor from a B-24. As photographer - gunner Bill Moran from the 90th BG, 321st BS put it: This was not the easiest of jobs, particularly with flak and fighter interception. From a photographers point of view, it was an understatement. At 21,000 feet, hovering over an open hatch, wind blowing in your eyes, sometimes tears running down your face, trying to balance a 24-inch cone camera, encumbered with heavy flying suits....". One begins top appreciate the difficulty in obtaining these photographs. As one wit in the 90th BG was quoted as sayiing: "When the ack-ack starts, you can be sure you've found your target."* (John Stava Collection)

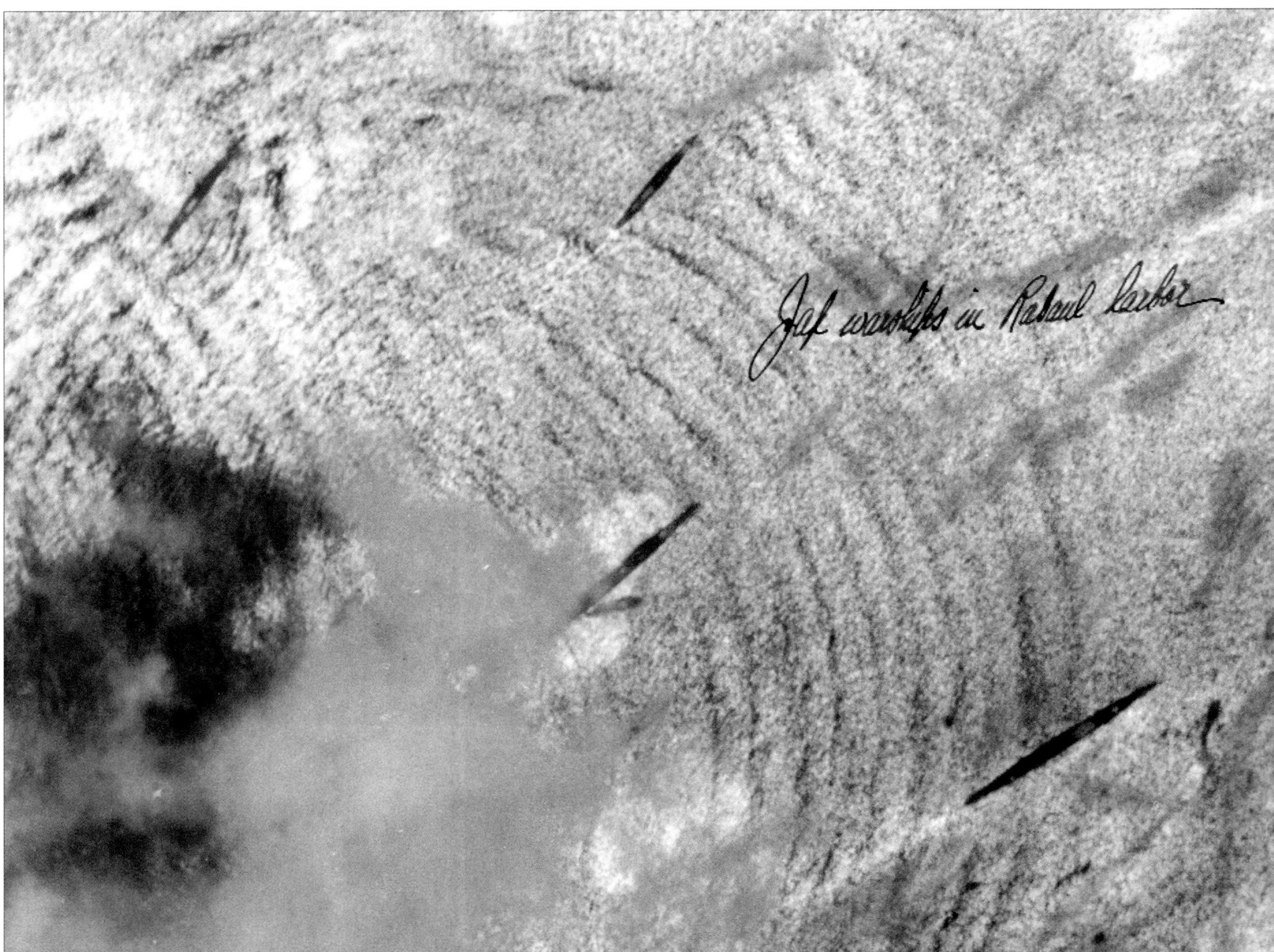

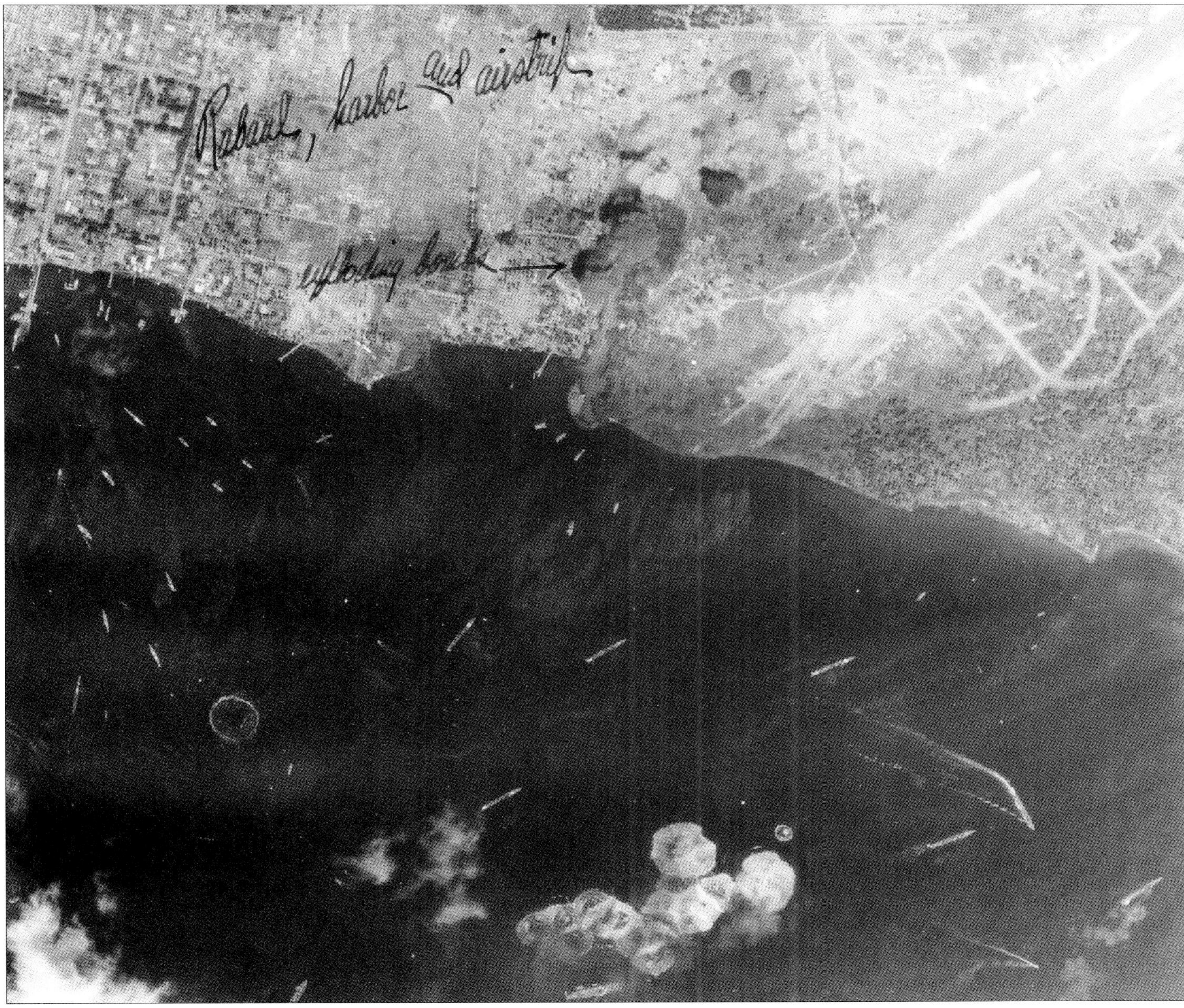

"Mission to Rabaul; Rabaul was the Jap fortress of the Pacific. Everyone knew that for a brief time, they would be flying into the jaws of hell"

-Vic Tatelman, 499th BS, 345 BG

(Above) *Another view of the attack unfolding over Rabaul. Caption on the back reads "Bomb bursts on A/A positions at Rabaul." This photos on this and the previous page were most likely taken on the October 12th Raid. The airfield in the upper right corner is Lukanai. The top of the photo is facing east Many USAAF flyers commented that Rabaul was an aromatic place - between the sulpher of the volvanoes and the cordite from the AA guns. There was even one bizarre mission earlier in the year where a 1,000 lb bomb was dropped down the mouth of one of the two volcanos surrounding the city in a hopes of jumpstarting an eruption, with no effect. Mother nature would handle that job with a double eruption in September of 1994.* (John Stava Collection)

(Right) *This is what it looks like when they are firing flak up at you. Fortunately their aim appears top be off, from this photo. According to an article written by Robert Cromie of the Chicago Tribune on Oct. 14th, 1943, one dialogue on the plane he was flying in went :"Don't bomb the geisha houses" some one yelled. "Why not?" a companion asked. "You can kill more Japs there than anywhere else. "Yeah," the first speaker said, "but the last time we did they got awfully mad." Cromie was flying along in a B-24 "Satan's Sister" on the October 12th raid.* (John Stava Collection)

(Above) *Strafing run through Simpson Harbor during the November 2nd raid. 3rd BG Pilot "Jock" Henebry had just run the gauntlet in his B-25 "Notre Dame de Victoire" placing a probable hit on the first ship (far right), the 4,217 ton Hokuyo Maru, and has scored a direct hit on the 10,380 ton Hakusan Maru (center). On his run the "Haguro", a "Nachi" class heavy cruiser to the left was firing her 8 inch guns at the attacking aircraft, hoping either the concussion or ensuing waterspouts would throw off the B25's aim and maybe put one or two in the water. In Jock's words: "Two strikes, two hits but now I had problems. The Haguro was in too close to the second transport, making it impossible to push the nose of the B-25 down fast enough to get my guns onto the deck and silence the fire. I had bellied up to the target and was fair game. The ship was firing at us, fire we couldn't return. I couldn't even drop my third bomb. I looked down and saw her gunners training their pom-pom guns to follow our flight path. They did hit us. And hard!" Henebry would manage to fly his crippled B-25 out of the battle, then fight off a Japanese fighter that would knock out his left engine, limping all the way to Kiriwina Island, where he would ditch near a coral reef where he and his crew would be picked up within hours by a patrolling PT boat that had spotted the crash.* (Photo courtesy of Marc Wiederwax)

(Below left) *Merchants in the harbor getting worked over by B-25's of the 3rd and 38th Bomber Groups. The photos on this page were submitted by Marc Wiederwax, the son of Dick Wiederwax from the 5th AF Photo Lab. Like my uncle, Dick Wiederwax was flying on these missions as a combat photographer. He was credited with one probable on this date and two the following day.* (Photo courtesy of Marc Wiederwax)

(Below right) *One of the defensive tactics tried by the Japanese at Rabaul was to have Ki-61 "Tony" Fighters drop aerial phospherous bombs down into American bomber formations. Visually interesting but not particularly effective.* (John Stava Collection)

(Opposite Top) *Another near miss in Simpson Harbor.* (Photo courtesy of Marc Wiederwax)

(Opposite Bottom) *A 71st Squadron 38th B.G. B-25 runs the gauntlet in Simpson Harbor while the Rabaul township burns fiercely in the background.* (National Archives)

"Any person who pretended (and some did) that he did not feel cold, penetrating fear at such a time was either abnormal or he was an outrageous liar."

-Garrett Middlebrook, Air Combat at 20 Feet

"The smoke from our 8 machine guns filled the cockpit and made vision difficult. About half way across the Harbor, I became aware that there were no B-25s to my left where there had been three just a few moments earlier."

-William Webster, 8th BS, 3rd BG

(Opposite Top and Bottom) *A Nakajima J1N1" Irving" (Gekko) nightfighter from the 251st* Kokutai *attempts to take off during the attack at Lakunai airfield with Simpson Harbor in the background. The "Irving" was Japan's first effective night-fighter and many of their tactics would be honed here at Rabaul. It was equipped with a pair of upward and downward firing 20mm cannon. Initially deemed ridiculous by the Japanese Naval GHQ, it soon proved it's worth against American night raids until the USAAF got wise and stuck to daylight raids. Rabaul's "King of the Night", PO1/c Shigetoshi Kudo would establish his career here in the "Irving". These photos were taken by a 345th BG, 501st BS B-25 on the November 2nd raid.* (Photos courtesy of Marc Wiederwax)

(Top) *Parafrags float down over parked "Betty" bombers at Lukunai Airdrome during the November 2nd raid. Note the "Zeke" fighter with the folding wing tips. Shortly after phosphorous bombs from the 499th Sq, 345th BG would wipe out these planes.*

(Bottom) *Another view of Vunakanau Airdrome getting carpeted with bombs. Simpson Harbor can be seen off in the distance.* (Photo courtesy of Marc Wiederwax)

(Top) *More paragfrags waft down near Sulpher Creek near the revetment of this Ki-45' 'Nick'. Note the abandoned fuel trucks.* (National archives)

(Right) *Recon shot of AA positions at Vunakanau airfield. Ian Quinn, a retired British Airways pilot who lived many years in the area mentioned that until the 1990's much of this site was still there, including the Shinto Shrine and AA positions. A Zero fighter sat nearby in the jungle until recently.* (John Stava Collection)

(OppositeTop) *More paragfrags floating down over Betty's in their revements at Vunakanau. The Japanese embankments were too low to adequately protect thier aircraft, something the Americans could never figure out.* (John Stava Collection)

(Opposite Bottom) *Three Ki-61 "Tony" Fighters sit complacently in their revetments while in the background the main concrete strip at Vunakanau takes a pounding. Nearly 6 miles from Simpson harbor, Vunakanau at the time was the most developed airdrome in the Rabaul area with it's concrete runways. Today only traces of it remain.* (John Stava Collection)

VUNAKANAU

1943 Cleanup

As the year drew to a close the Japanese forces in eastern New Guinea we're either in retreat, neutralized, or wiped out. The 5th Air Force had established a major base at Nadzab and was well poised to begin it's leap frog campaign westward along the New Guinea coast as a lead in to retaking the Philippines. December would see the invasion of western part of New Britain at Cape Gloucester after an unprecedented bombardment by medium and heavy bombers. The destruction was so complete that it entered the 5th A.F.'s vernacular as "Gloucesterizing". The effect was so complete that the Allied landing forces went ashore "standing up" as the stunned Japanese defences was so light and ineffective.

(Below) *New B-25G's arriving in the later part of 1943 came equipped with a whopping 75mm canon in the nose, which could be put to devistating effect as shown by this photo. However, it's slow rate of fire allowed only 3 -4 rounds to be fired on an attack run and the recoil was hell on the airframe - loosening rivets and even bending the airframe. The canon itself was 9 feet long and was reasonably accurate, although when it fired the some crews claimed the plane pretty much stopped in mid-air from the recoil and inexperienced crew were known to toss their cookies as well. Unpopular with flying and maintenance crews alike, most of the 75mm canon were scrapped in the field and the slot replaced with a more managable and effective 20mm cannon or an additional .50 caliber machine gun.* (John Stava Collection)

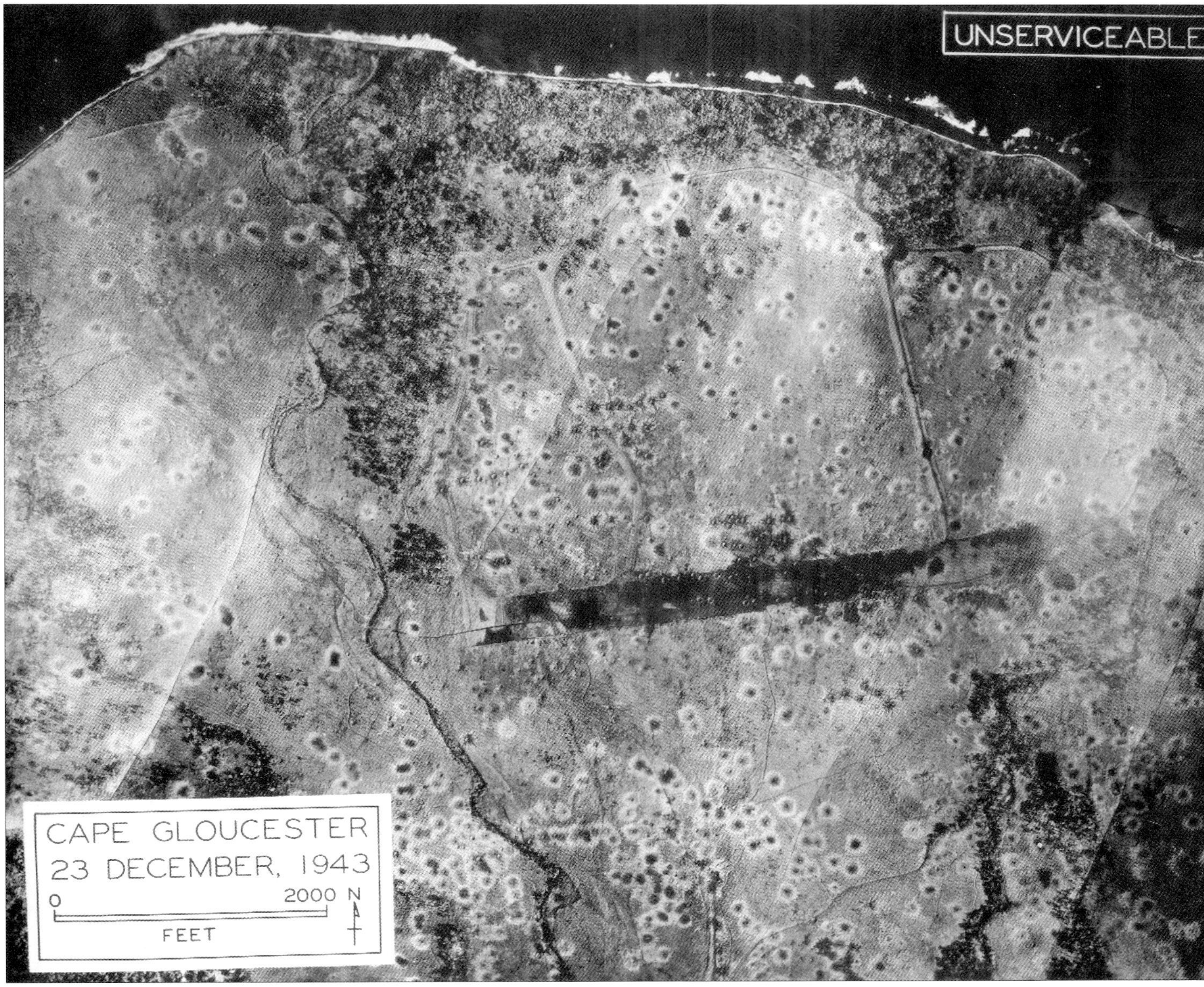

(Above) *This is what they mean by "Gloucesterizing". You take an enemy airbase, bomb the hell out of it until it looks like the surface of the moon.* (John Stava Collection)

(Below Left) *The same airfield in a well known photo in the early stages of the attack.* (National Archives)

(Below Right) *A 38th BG B-25 hits the coastline at Gloucester shortly after the naval bombardment.* (National Archives)

Wewak Area

February 3rd 1944 saw the 345th Bomber Group pummeling Dagua airdrome once again. In January the 5th had focused on two airdromes down the road, Wewak and Boram, to lull the Japanese into thinking Dagua and But were safe. The ruse worked and B-25's arriving on February 3rd found that the Japanese, according to General Kenney, "Behaved perfectly and had his planes lined up nicely, most of them with their engines turning over, crews in their seats and mechanics standing by". Though a fraction of the air strength these airdromes had been in 1943, between Dagua and But the 5th still destroyed 60 aircraft on the ground with another 16 falling to escorting fighters.

The Japanese stronghold in Northeast New Guinea, the 20 mile string of airdromes - Wewak, Boram, But, and Dagua - were basically knocked out of the picture after this last raid, their personal abandoned by the Japanese High Command who moved their 4th Army Headquarters up the coast to Hollandia and Tadji. By summer Wewak was being used for target practice by newly arriving 5th AF crews.

Captain's Hugh and Arnold had this more fanciful description of a Dagua raid in"Big Distance": "The Jap airstrip was packed with planes, concentrated there for a big strike at the Americans and ready to take off. The big .50 caliber bullets came in suddenly, like slanting hail, then the fast attacking bombers came in low behind their fire, like blackbirds in migration, swooping and fanning out over the reedtips of a marsh...."

(Below) *This often printed picture is still an amazing moment in time when one studies it. The Kawasaki Ki-61 "Tony's" lined up neatly on the runway as if for inspection amidst the parafrag bombs raining down on them is almost surreal. This photo was taken by Major Marston's B-25 "Wolf Pack"of the 345th BG, 501st Squadron. On the left is "The Eager Beaver" flown by 2nd Lt. Milton Harper and on the right "Meany" flown by 1st Lt. Richard A. Barth. The Kid-61 fighters are from the 78th Sentai, which was basically wiped out in New Guinea. While this photo has been occasionally mislabeled over the years, this original copy in John Stava's collection leaves little doubt as to the date or location.* (John Stava Collection)

(Opposite Top) *Another photo of the same raid showing Kid-43 Oscars and Kid-61 Tony fighters lined up with a couple of Kid-49 "Helen" Bombers. At least some of these aircraft appear to be derelict.* (John Stava Collection)

(Opposite Bottom) *Another photo from the 345th raid at Dagua on February 3rd, this one a close up of three abandoned fuel trucks near a camouflaged revetment hiding a Kid-43 "Oscar" of the 59th Sentai. The open doors of the trucks are almost a comic statement - "we're out of here" - of course when your enemy showed up in machine-gun packed strafers you didn't want to be caught sitting in a vehicle loaded with high-octane fuel. Shortly after this photo was taken the trucks would be set on fire.* (John Stava Collection)

DAGUA

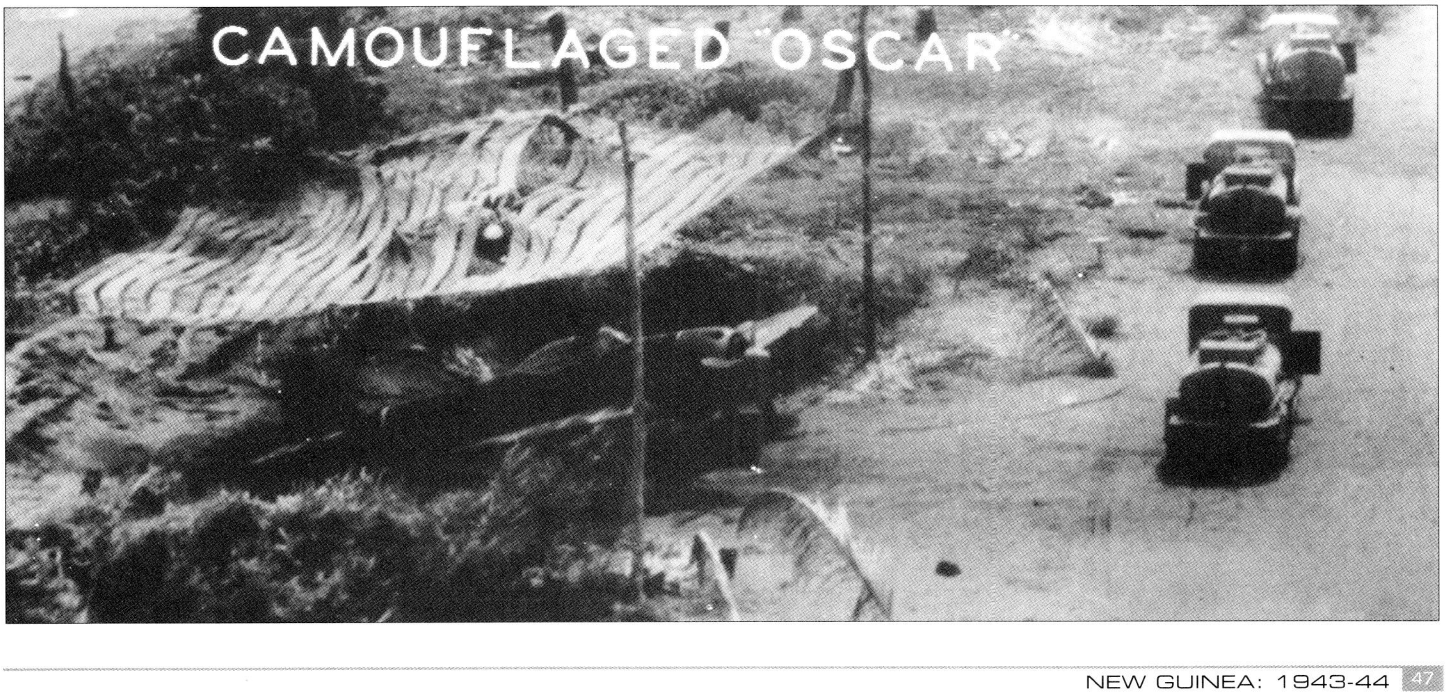
CAMOUFLAGED "OSCAR"

(Above) *An amazing shot captured this lugger a split second away from it's ultimate destruction. A textbook case in what happens when you drop a 500 lb bomb square on a small boat.* (John Stava Collection)

(Left) *Another Sally bomber gets caught unawares.* (John Stava Collection)

(Above) *Dramatic view of the attack on one of the ships from a convoy that tried to sneak into beleaguered Wewak on March 19th, 1944. 62 B-25s and A-20s and 40 B-24's escorted by 28 P-38's wiped out the convoy of 3 transports and 3 escorting corvette's. The demise of one of the transports is detailed on page 55.* (John Stava Collection)

(Right) *A view of the mission at Wewak. Note the white crosses painted on the roof indicating it is being used as a hospital. The Japanese placed several heavy AA gun positions right next to it, possibly playing on the Allied reluctance to bomb a Hospital. Hospital or not, the Americans finally let them have it (see page 52).* (John Stava Collection)

Long Distance Trip

The excerpt from John Stava's papers below tells the bare bones of the story; on February 25th 1944 a mission was assembled for a lone B-24 to make a recon run to Woleai Island (spelled then as "Waleai" in the document) located in the Carolinas Northwest of Truk to gather intelligence on the Japanese base there prior to a Naval attack planned in March. Lt. Vineyard and his crew from the 90th Bomber Group "Jolly Rogers" were originally slated to fly the mission but Major Paul Gottke, the 320th Squadron Commander, decided to fly it himself and bumped Vineyard to the co-pilots position, also bringing along his own navigators, Lieutenants Harlow and Davis. John Stava was assigned as the missions photographer. Flying over 1,000 miles into enemy territory in a lone aircraft and finding such a small island in such a vast expanse was no small feat, particularly when your only map was a copy of a hand drawn Russian whaler's map sketched in 1828 (Which, as it turned out was 60 miles from where it was indicated). At the briefing the Intelligence officer from 5th Bomber Command simply told the crew; *"Just find it boys, and take pictures of it and then come on home. It's a piece of cake, right?"*

Outside of a weather front lying across the Huon-Vitiaz area, which left the crew black and blue and some feed problems in the extra gas tanks installed in the bomb bay the trip was uneventful and they made several "leisurely" runs, with John taking 8 vertical and 19 oblique shots out the B-24's waist windows. Carl Camp, the right waist gunner and today the only surviving member who flew on the mission, recalled *"It also helped alot when the Jap flying boats* (Either H6K "Mavis" or H8K "Emily" Flying Boats) *in the lagoon mistook us for one of their own and they flashed us a green light to come on in and land on the lagoon instead of sending up some or all of the twenty fighters on the airstrip to bust our asses. While they were still thinking that we got the hell out of there. Sure it was a piece of cake, we were only scared shitless all the way there and half the way back."* The entire flight lasted 14 hours and 13 minutes.

Camp continued: *"The whole thing was a stacked deck. Major Gottke bumped Johnson from the right seat and moved Vinyard over to fly co-pilot. Since we were not going to be bombing, Grzesik (bombadier) was left at home and Gottke put his own old navigator, Harrington Harlow, to 'help' ours. Both the bastards already had a Distinguished Flying Cross but they wanted another."*

"When we returned with the most beautiful pictures imaginable, Gottke put himself, Harlow and Davis in for the Distinguished Flying Cross and us peasants including Vineyard and your uncle only got an Air Medal. We either all deserved the DFC or nothing at all...I caught up with him (Gottke) at a reunion years later and gave him hell for it."

Camp had one last remark: *"That flight was one other thing. At 14 hours it was the longest combat flight I ever made."*

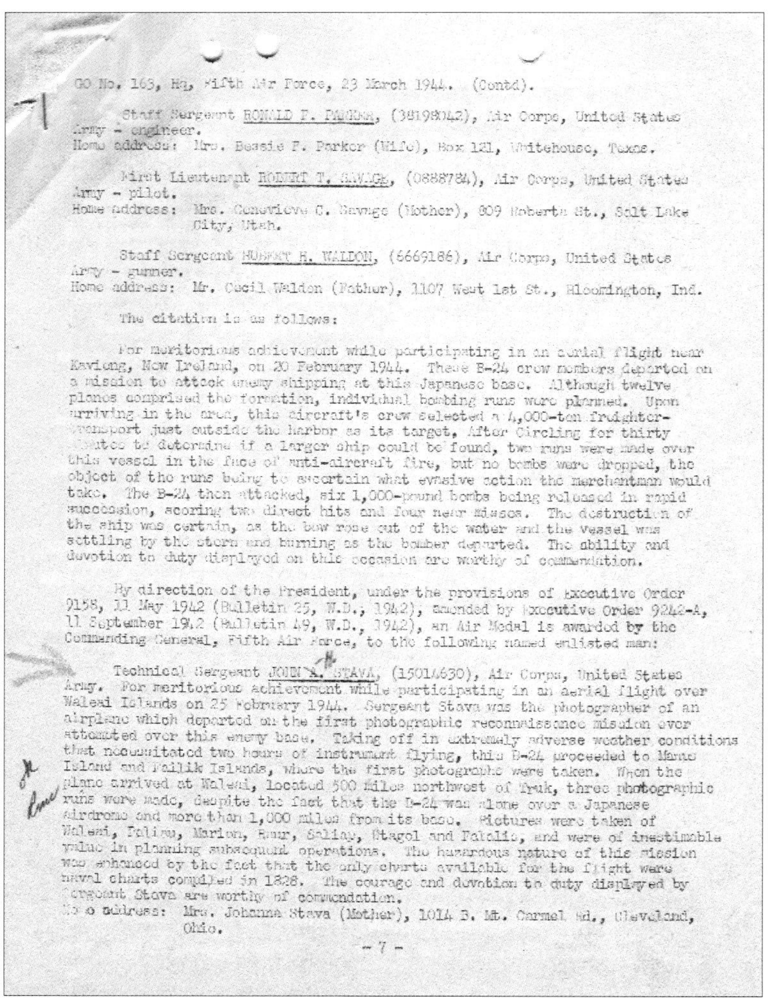

GO No. 163, Hq, Fifth Air Force, 23 March 1944. (Contd).

Staff Sergeant RONALD F. PARKER, (38198042), Air Corps, United States Army - engineer.
Home address: Mrs. Bessie F. Parker (Wife), Box 121, Whitehouse, Texas.

First Lieutenant ROBERT T. SAVAGE, (0888784), Air Corps, United States Army - pilot.
Home address: Mrs. Genevieve C. Savage (Mother), 809 Roberts St., Salt Lake City, Utah.

Staff Sergeant HUBERT H. WALDON, (6669186), Air Corps, United States Army - gunner.
Home address: Mr. Cecil Waldon (Father), 1107 West 1st St., Bloomington, Ind.

The citation is as follows:

For meritorious achievement while participating in an aerial flight near Kavieng, New Ireland, on 20 February 1944. These B-24 crew members departed on a mission to attack enemy shipping at this Japanese base. Although twelve planes comprised the formation, individual bombing runs were planned. Upon arriving in the area, this aircraft's crew selected a 4,000-ton freighter-transport just outside the harbor as its target. After Circling for thirty minutes to determine if a larger ship could be found, two runs were made over this vessel in the face of anti-aircraft fire, but no bombs were dropped, the object of the runs being to ascertain what evasive action the merchantman would take. The B-24 then attacked, six 1,000-pound bombs being released in rapid succession, scoring two direct hits and four near misses. The destruction of the ship was certain, as the bow rose out of the water and the vessel was settling by the stern and burning as the bomber departed. The ability and devotion to duty displayed on this occasion are worthy of commendation.

By direction of the President, under the provisions of Executive Order 9158, 11 May 1942 (Bulletin 25, W.D., 1942), amended by Executive Order 9242-A, 11 September 1942 (Bulletin 49, W.D., 1942), an Air Medal is awarded by the Commanding General, Fifth Air Force, to the following named enlisted man:

Technical Sergeant JOHN A. STAVA, (15014630), Air Corps, United States Army. For meritorious achievement while participating in an aerial flight over Waleai Islands on 25 February 1944. Sergeant Stava was the photographer of an airplane which departed on the first photographic reconnaissance mission over attempted over this enemy base. Taking off in extremely adverse weather conditions that necessitated two hours of instrument flying, this B-24 proceeded to Manus Island and Failik Islands, where the first photographs were taken. When the plane arrived at Waleai, located 500 miles northwest of Truk, three photographic runs were made, despite the fact that the B-24 was alone over a Japanese airdrome and more than 1,000 miles from its base. Pictures were taken of Waleai, Falipu, Marion, Raur, Saliap, Utagol and Falalis, and were of inestimable value in planning subsequent operations. The hazardous nature of this mission was enhanced by the fact that the only charts available for the flight were naval charts compiled in 1828. The courage and devotion to duty displayed by Sergeant Stava are worthy of commendation.
Home address: Mrs. Johanna Stava (Mother), 1014 E. Mt. Carmel Rd., Cleveland, Ohio.

- 7 -

(Left) *Citation report from John Stava's records awarding him his first Air Medal. The entire crew for the mission was: Major Gottke (Pilot), Lt. Carl H. Vineyard jr. (co-pilot), Lt. Harrington Harlow (navigator), Lt. Richard E. Davis (Navigator/bombardier, Sgt. Van R. Holloway (Engineer), Sgt. Leo G. Bousquet (Gunner), Sgt. Carl D. Camp (Gunner), Sgt. Albert C. Hampton (Gunner), Sgt. Stanley E. Horton (Radio Operator), Sgt. Elmer F. Wimer (Gunner), John Stava (Photographer).* (John Stava Collection)

(Above) *Major Paul Gottke pokes his head out the pilot's window of "Moby Dick", the B-24 he usually flew.* (photo courtesy of Robert Tupa)

(Opposite top and middle left) *Two of the photos John took of that mission of Woleai Atoll. Carl recalled: "We spent about 15 minutes flubbing around that island group while your uncle took pictures out the waist window while the rest of us were silently urging him to hurry up so we could drag ass home". Even today these islands are very difficult to access, requiring special permits that take months of waiting. When I asked if any of the enemy fighters came up after them, Carl replied "No! Must have been their tea hour."* (Courtesy of Carl Camp)

(Middle right) *Carl Camp strikes a pose in front of a Japanese cemetery near Nadzab.* (Courtesy of Carl Camp)

(Opposite Bottom) *Vineyards crew usually flew on this B-24, No. 095. The actual B-24 flown on the mission was unnamed, No. M-810.* (photo courtesy of Carl Camp)

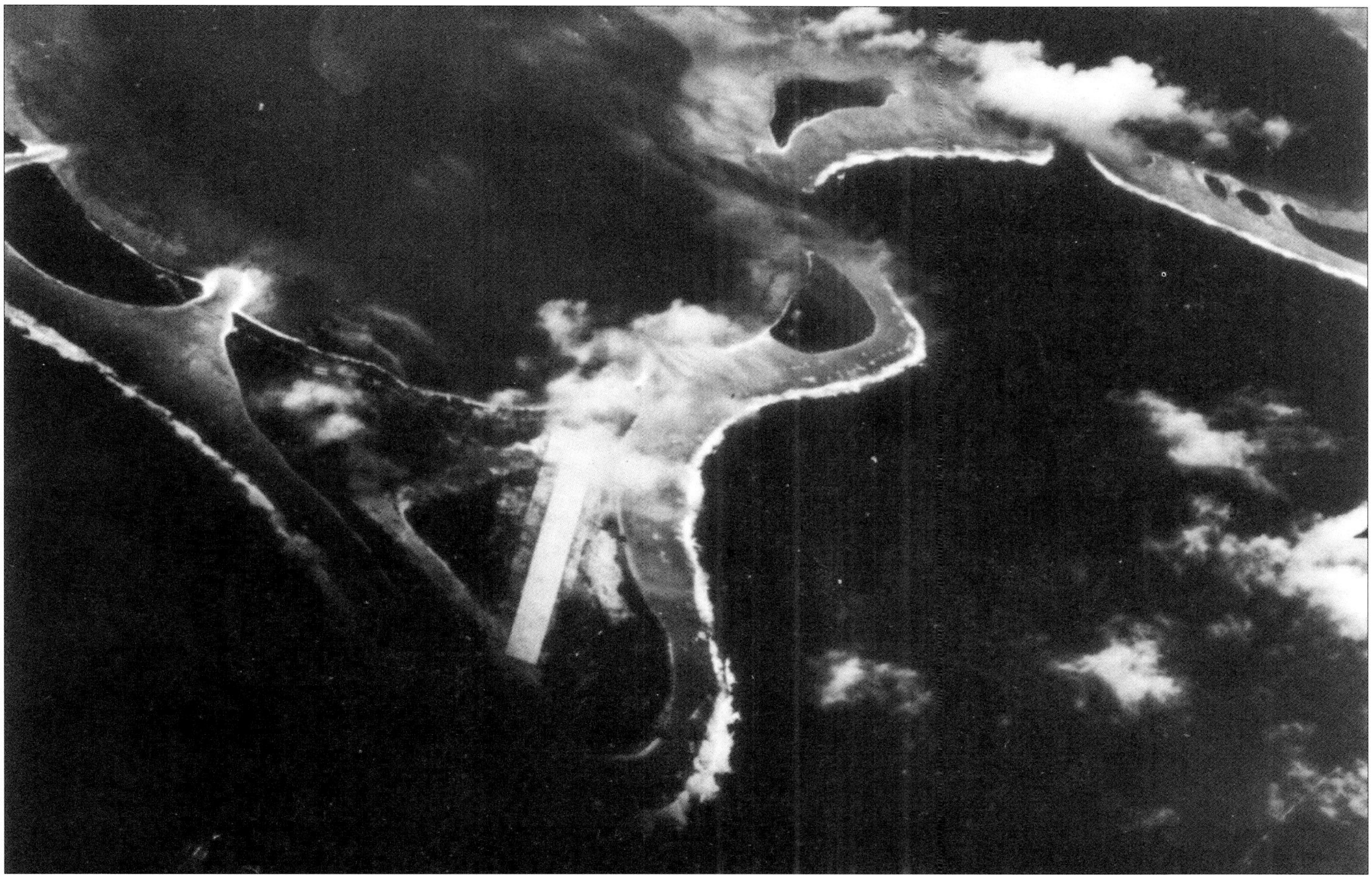

JAPANESE WAR CEMETERY

WEWAK STRIKE
15 MARCH 1944
DESTROYED
WEWAK MISSION
4 GUN H A/A
FIRE CONTROL
BURNING AIRPLANE

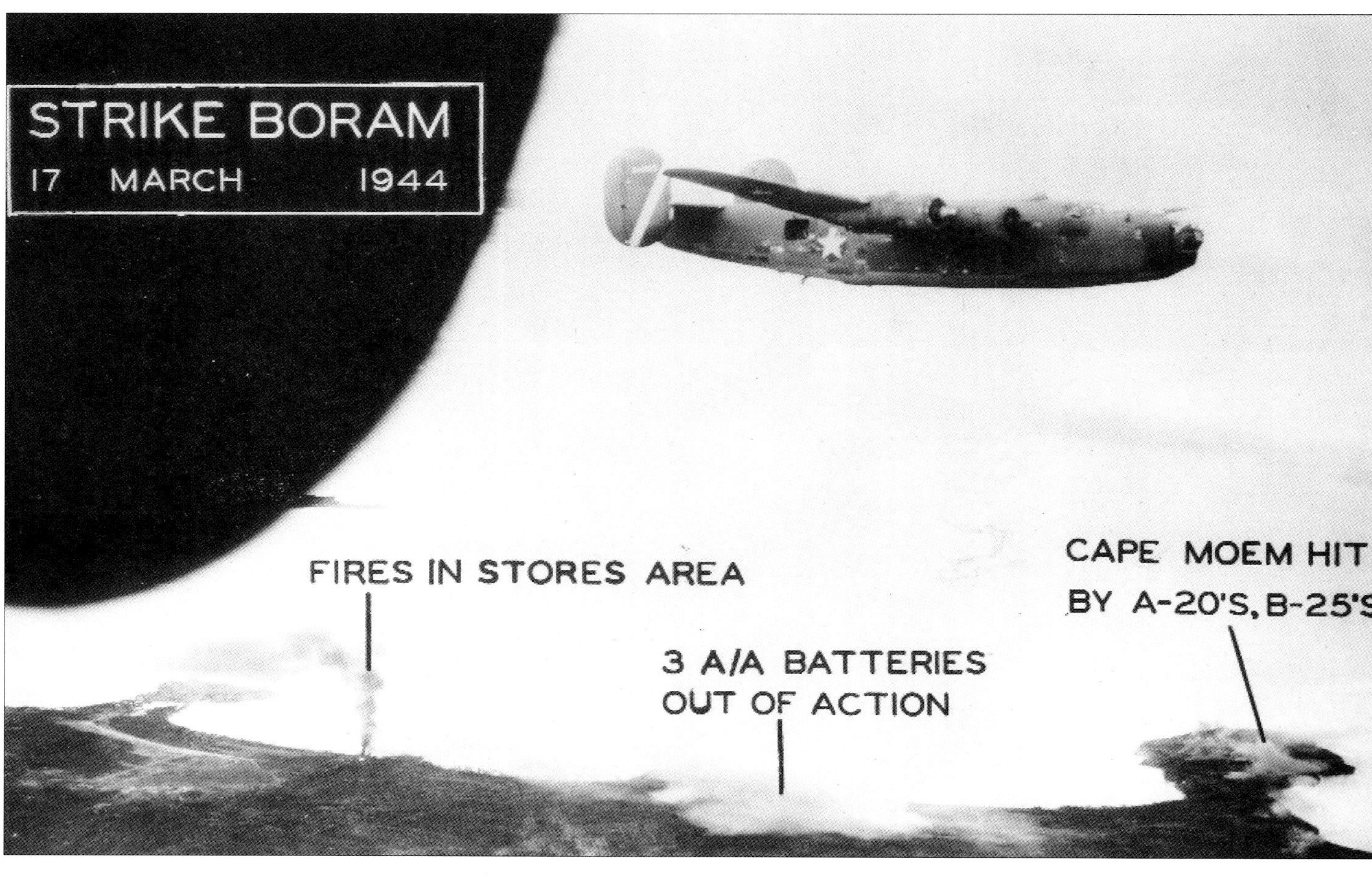
STRIKE BORAM
17 MARCH 1944
FIRES IN STORES AREA
CAPE MOEM HIT
BY A-20'S, B-25'S
3 A/A BATTERIES
OUT OF ACTION

(Opposite Top and Bottom) *B-24 Liberators of the 43rd Bomber Group, 64th Squadron make the rounds over the Wewak area. Note in the upper photo the Wewak Mission, seen in the photo on page 45. In this photo the Allies have gotten around to blasting the heavy AA positions next to the hospital. From this photo it appears the hospital won't be accepting new patients anytime soon.* (John Stava Collection)

(Below) *Recon shot from the March 16th Raid.*(John Stava Collection)

345th at New Hanover

Early on the morning of February 16th, 1944 forty-one B-25's of the 345th BG joined up with three squadrons from the 38th BG to track down a 14 ship Japanese convoy reportedly heading for Kavieng. The convoy wasn't found but a tanker and patrol boat were, just off the west coast of New Hanover, a large island just west of Kavieng on New Ireland. The tanker, the 5,461 ton Sanko Maru, was destroyed quickly by 500 pound bombs and a "midget sub" parked alongside it severely damaged. Meanwhile the other Japanese ship - Subchaser #39 - took off in a frenzy of violent maneuvers while being bracketed by 500 pound bombs only to run aground on a shallow reef nearby. The B-25's went in for the kill and shortly the ships boiler blew, hurling several chunks of debris right through the rear fuselage of "Lucky Bat" who happened to be passing over at the moment.

About 40 sailors escaped the carnage only to be strafed in the water by subsequent passes until the water was red. Only a few wounded stragglers made it to shore.

(Below) *Another often reprinted image, it still is a fascinating moment when pauses to study the details. This photo was taken by 500 BS B-25 "Rita's Wagon" piloted by Capt. Max Mortensen. The crew of "Rita's Wagon" would go on to pull of one of the more ambitious practical jokes of the war when they scrapped together a steel kitchen sink and actually dropped it ("everything including the kitchen sink") on a Japanese airdrome at Sidate during a bomb run in Celebes on September 19th, 1944. The B-25 with the shark mouth in the photo is "Brother Rat" flown by Lt. Richard Fitzshall. Neither plane has scored a direct hit with their bombs at this point. One can be seen falling by the water geyser upper left. Note the crewman still manning the 75mm AA gun on the front deck while two more run belowdecks to the right as another seems to be hugging the bridge superstrucvture. 499th Bomber Squadron pilot Capt. Vic Tatelman recalled that day: "I do remember that the Japs ran their ship onto the beach with the sailors jumping into the water trying to get to the beach. One of our airplanes circled around and strafed that line of Jap sailors, but I don't recall what aircraft that was."* (John Stava Collection)

(Above) *Another photo of Subchaser #39 on her ill-fated run. A small fire has begun in the aft section and the forward 75mm has been abandoned. Several crewmen can be seen huddling near the rail. I asked 345th Pilot Vic Tatelman how he dealt with flying into combat and he replied: "The fear was palpable, building all along the route to the target, but I found it manageable by talking to the crew. If I could keep my voice calm asking for feedback, keeping each crew member fixed on his assigned task. The really amazing part of that fear, when the target appeared, or even when the first bursts of anti-aircraft fire were seen ahead, the fear disappeared entirely replaced by calm deliberation, concentration, knowing exactly what my position in the formation was to be flown. And when we turned into the target, Willie, my co-pilot, put his hands on the yoke and feet on the rudder pedals; he knew if I was hit, there wouldn't be time for him to take control otherwise. His calmness and cool underfire was a plus for all of us; all that smoke and noise, machine gun fire, bombs exploding, Jap anti-aircraft bursts, and keeping an eye on the aircraft beside you, can't allow any drift, could be catastrophic. Then the target exit, form up quickly, defensive fire immediate, the Jap fighter attacks came swiftly at that point."* (John Stava Collection)

(Below left and right) *The previous day the 5th Air Force had send the 345th and 38th Bomber Groups to work over the Japanese supply base at Kavieng in a devastating low-level raid. The 345th alone lost four B-25s on this mission either to AA fire or flying debris from an exploding fuel dump. The flying 55 gallon gasoline drums from the ensuing explosions seemed to be as hazardous to the attackers as the AA batteries, several were seen sailing up past through the formations, one which clipped B-25 "Mexican Spitfire" on it's outboard wing.* (John Stava Collection)

When Mitch met Sally

Although bomber to bomber air battles weren't common, they did happen. On February 25th, 1944 this Japanese Mitsubishi Ki-21 "Sally" bomber had an unfortunate run in with the 17th Recon's B-25 "Mitch The Witch", flown by Captain Bert Still, near Kavieng, New Ireland. Sill had been on a recon patrol strafing luggers in the East Bismarck Sea and was flying at 1,000 feet when he spotted this Sally at 3,000 feet heading for Rabaul at around 230 mph. Sill's plane made seven passes - not the affectionate kind - for four minutes from above, below and the side until both engines of the Sally finally caught fire and she plunged into the ocean. Upon impact the tail section broke off and the aircraft burst into a huge flame before sinking to her watery grave. All five crewmen were presumed to have perished before impact.

John would serve under Capt. Sill later on when he signed up with the 17th Recon officially in the fall of 1944 and Sill was by then operations officer. Like all the crews in the 17th he would also fly his share of missions on "Mitch The Witch" as well.

Although already obsolete at the time of the Pearl Harbor attack, the Ki-21 Type 97 heavy bomber remained a staple of the Japanese Army Air Force's bomber squadrons throughout the war.

(Below, Opposite Far Right and Bottom) *"Mitch the Witch" takes on a Mitsubishi Ki-21 "Sally". The bombers' light 7.7 machines guns were no match for the B-25's .50 calibers* (John Stava Collection)

(Above) *Bertram Sill, 17th Recon Operations officer. He would command the 17th Recon right up to the end of the war, often flying combat missions. He would wind up ditching his B-25 during the December 26th 1944 mission described later in this book. He was also a top Bridge player, the card game of choice amongst 17th Recon personnel.* (Photo from "Strike!", History of the 17th)

Enemy Aircraft

Somewhere along the way the Photo Lab team must have had some spare time on their hands and threw together these somewhat crude - by today's digital retouching standards - photo montages of enemy aircraft in the S.W.P.A. The photos are a hodgepodge of images from Rabaul, Wewak, and Hollandia so that would probably date them around mid to late summer of 1944. The 5th Air Force Advon Photo lab worked closely with the 2nd AAF Photo Intelligence Detachment - the later would have been responsible for analyzing the photographic content, and shortly after the 5th AF had moved up to the Philippines both groups were merged into one as with the war moving into it's final phase less personnel were deemed necessary. By early 1945 many of the original Photo Lab team like Fred Miller and Bob Crowe were allowed to return home, while John continued as a tail gunner with the 17th Recon. Bob Crowe recalled that while in the Philippines John would drop by the photo lab for a visit and that he seemed "much happier" now that he was in a full time combat squadron. Crowe's thoughts on this were "Well, you have to understand that some people like your uncle may have had felt guilt over their jobs in the lab. Being with HQ we had it pretty easy compared to most of the guys - being with Bomber Command we were a ways back from the danger and had the best food, lodgings, safety, and some may not have felt like they were really doing their part like the guys in the front line were. I didn't have that problem."

(Opposite Page, this page top and Bottom) *Montages of assorted Japanese aircraft created for the Intelligence section, possibly disctrubuted for identification uses. The ki-49 "Tony" fighter above was initially mistaken by Allied pilots for the German Me109 when it first appeared in combat. It earned it's nickname from it's resemblance to the Italian Macchi C.202* (John Stava Collection)

A20 Attack March 19th

The dramatic photo below has been staple fare in many books on the 5th AF, but the subsequent sequence of photos chronicling the ship's destruction is rarely seen. On the morning of March 19th, 1944 a Japanese resupply convoy was caught sneaking out off the coast of Wewak after unloading supplies the night before and pounded by B-25's and A-20's of the 345th BG and 3rd BG respectively. What followed was a maelstrom of destruction as the the three bomber groups attacked in swarms disregarding the risk of collision, leaving the ocean littered with surviviors and debris. In the photo below this A20 Havoc of the 89th Squadron has just hit the mast of the freighter and crashed into the ocean shortly after. The gunner, Sgt. Donald Bradley went down with the plane but the pilot, Lt. Soloc, survived and was picked up by a Catalina after 17 hours in the drink. Within minutes the ship would be a minor footnote in history, little more than bits of floating debris to mark her passing. The bottom two photos opposite show the remains as well as a few survivors. The .50 calibers of the 345th's B25's would make short work of them in subsequent satrafing passes. Mercy in the combat zone was often hinged on a whim. One day a strafer pilot and his crew might feel a twinge of compassion for his enemy and leave him to the fates, on another day the same pilot might decide to vent his rage on his foe by gunning him down. It may sound "unsporting" to some that our air crews would kill a helpless enemy floating in the water but this was war and at the time the hatred between our respective countries ran deep. Certainly the Japanese had no issue returning the gesture.

In a subsequent odd turn of events, another A-20 pilot on this mission, Lt. Rade Vukelic also of the 89th Sq., found a scrap of paper jammed into one of the engine cowlings of his plane after returning to base. It turned out to be a page from the ships log revealing the name and tonnage of the ship - the 3,221-ton freighter Taiei Maru - which had been blasted out of the bridge by a direct bomb hit while he was passing over. The Lieutenant decided to have a little fun with the intelligence officers at his debriefing and proceeded to drive them nuts by describing the target right down to the exact name and tonnage until finally owning up and passing over the document saying, "It's proof, isn't it?"

(Below and Opposite Page,) *This sequence of photos ranks amongst the most intense ever captured in the Southwest Pacific theater and underscores how dangerous low-level shipping strikes were for the aircraft as well as the ships.* (John Stava Collection)

Hollandia 1944

By March of 1944 Hollandia had become the major Japanese Air Base in New Guinea. With the Wewak airstrips effectively knocked out of the picture by March 16th, the Japanese began a massive build up at Hollandia, convinced it was, for the moment, outside the range of American fighter escort and convinced that the Allies would focus on invading the Wewak area. Which was exactly what Kenney was gambling on. In fact, the 5th had ditched it's plan to invade Wewak. Instead their strategy was to get the Japanese to concentrate their Air Forces at Hollandia, then blitz the airfields there in a week long series of massive attacks, then launch a surprise invasion at Hollandia and Aitape - a secondary base almost halfway between Hollandia and Wewak on the northern coast. The whole effort was carefully planned by intercepting and monitoring Japanese communications.

The ploy worked. On the morning of March 30th 689 B-24s with P-38 fighter escort hit Hollandia with parafrag bombs, targeting the antiaircraft positions and the fuel dumps. The next day the 5th heavies put on a repeat performance - within those two days nearly 200 Japanese aircraft would be destroyed on the ground. When the weather again cleared on April 3rd, the 5th opted to really put some elbow grease into it and launched their most massive strike to date - sixty-three B-24s opened the ceremonies with heavy bombs, followed by ninety-six A20s who slow-rolled over the hills and blitzed the three airstrips, followed by a clean-up crew at noon of B-25s who swept the area with parafrag and parademo bombs. The result would be the end of Japanese air power in New Guinea. The amount of destruction was staggering - entire squadrons ceased to exist, ground personnel would be abandoned by Japanese High Command and left to walk up the coast to the nearest friendly bases.

Two weeks later the Allied invasion would arrive but there was little in the way of resistance.

(Below) *Probably taken from a B-24, aerial view of the March 31st raid.* (Opposite Top) *Dramatic shot of a 312th BG A-20 Havoc coming in low and fast on the April 3rd raid.* (John Stava Collection)

(Opposite Bottom) *Not much left - another low level run from the April 3rd mission. A derelect Ki48 "Lily" is in the foreground.* (John Stava Collection)

"Planes sometimes tried to go through trees instead of around them; the distance above the jungle was easy to misjudge, when it came down to a matter of feet and even inches; wing-tips touched the ground on sharp turns....the results, so clear and decisive, were paid for, in the end, by the people who flew the airplanes."

- Capt. Donald Hough and Capt Elliott Arnold, "Big Distance"

(Right) *Another low level shot from April 3rd.* (John Stava Collection)

(Bottom) *A Japanese Mitsubishi Ki-46 "Dinah" bomber gets the parafrag "makeover".* (John Stava Collection)

(Oppposite Top & Bottom) *Little more to add here - Johns notes on the photos pretty much sums it up.* (John Stava Collection)

Burning Nip planes after strafing
at Hollandia

Destruction of Hollandia
278 Nip planes destroyed
on ground in 2 days

Summertime Blues

(Opposite page) A Japanese freighter get's the up close and personal treatment from B-25s of the 823rd Squadron, 38th Bomber Group in the Sarong area, New Guinea on June 17th 1944. This dramatic shot shows clearly what .50 caliber machine guns do to a ship and underscores just how low they flew on these strafing runs. As 38th BG Pilot Garrett Middlebrook put it "Timid pilots did not live long in our deadly game of air combat at 20 feet." The bottom photo is the same ship after it beached. Bodies can be seen along the decks and in the water, although one sailor can be seen standing by the aft deck cannon, either defiant or shell-shocked or both. (John Stava Collection)

(Below) The two ships in the background have been obliterated and the one in the foreground is looking to follow shortly after A-20's of the 3rd Bomber Group, 13th Squadron dropped by for a visit at Manokwari, New Guinea on June 9th, 1944. (John Stava Collection)

(Left) A 312th BG A20 Havoc emerges from roiling thunderheads of burning oil from storage tanks at Boela, Ceram on July 15th, 1944. Boela was a major oil center for the Japanese located on the easter end of Ceram, about 750 miles from Hollandia from where the attack was staged. The attack began with the 3rd BG taking the Japanese completely by surprise but by the time the 312th BG followed up on the second run the AA batteries were eager and willing, although of the attacking force of 75 planes only one A-20 was brought down. Smoke from the ruptered oil tanks rose up to 3,000 feet. A hallmark photo, it appears on the wall of John's office at Nadzab (see page 15) which dates that photo after that. (Robert Stava Collection)

Local Images II

(Opposite Page Clockwise from upper left) 1) *One of the more unusual shots in the collection, perhaps because it's so non-descript. I couldn't understand why this shot of a civilian by a 345th BG B25 was taken - until I realized that the gentleman dead center is none other than Charles Lindbergh. Probably taken at Nadzab, July 1944 when Lindbergh showed up in New Guinea to help P38 Pilots get more range through better fuel management. Lindbergh was a controversial figure at the time. Opposed to U.S. involvement with the situation in Europe, he visited Nazi Germany in a carefully staged tour that drew harsh criticism from President Roosevelt. After Pearl Harbor he started singing a different tune and offered his services to the Air Force, but Uncle Sam wasn't interested. Undaunted, Lindbergh eventually went to the South Pacific where he would fly with the 475th Fighter Group. Flying as a civilian, "Mr. Lindbergh" would shoot down a Japanese "Sally" over Ceram Island on July 28th of 1944, then nearly got himself shot down in an engagement four days later. With the first incident General Kenney turned a blind eye but the second one was too much and the plug was pulled on Lindberghs endeavors in the South Pacific. 2) Got to love those RayBans - John Stava looking sharp in aviator glasses. Bob Crowe noted that he was "quite a drinker" even by WWII standards and that he spent much of his time either in his bunk or in the lab, but that he always got the work done. He also told me that John flew combat missions quite frequently and never came back with his guns unfired - which may be a bit of a stretch but that's what the man said. 3) Written on the back of this photo in John's hand "This is the Red Cross gal who meets us when we return from missions and feeds us cold drinks and cookies - and in the lower left hand corner - a buddy of mine." 4) Not sure what he's up to with that machete, but Dick Wiederwax looks like he means business. Wiederwax was one of the original Photo Lab team but later transferred to an Air Sea rescue unit flying in PBY Catalina's. Bob Crowe described him as "Quite a character - always getting himself promoted, not in rank but onto special assignments like picking up supplies in Australia. He had a knack for finding women, like in Port Moresby, where nobody else could." Dick's nickname was "Jackson", as he was originally from Jackson, Michigan.* (Photos 1- 3, John Stava Collection, Photo #4 courtesy of Marc Wiederwax)

(Below) 1 & 2) *Someone with a sense of humor and a bit too much free time strung up this sign up over the road near the 5th AF Camp at Port Moresby - on the back John had written "This sign isn't kidding". Mosquitoes transmitting Malaria and Dengue Fever were a plague to our troops in New Guinea as well as the local populous - along the costal regions the infection rate for Malaria amongst native New Guinea's was around 100 percent.. 3 & 4) "This python which measured 12' crawled into one of our tents one night" it says on the back. It doesn't appear he was made to feel welcome. I like the guy on the far right trying to get in on the action by holding the very tip of the tail.* (John Stava Collection)

1.

2.

4.

3.

1.

2.

4.

3.

5th AF Brass

The 5th Air Force certainly had no shortage of colorful commanders. MacArthur had made a prudent choice in bringing in General George C. Kenney to take control of the 5th A.F. - he quickly set about cleaning house and getting rid of any dead weight and made a point of putting capable men in capable positions. Not much in the way of a political game player, Kenney was about getting the job done in the most efficient way possible. His choice of second in command, General Ennis C. Whitehead, was a prime example of this. Whitehead was given command of the Advanced Echelon of 5th AF HQ - basically the forward command arm - and had the authority to make his own command decisions on the fly to adapt to the changing front line situation, which kept the 5th AF fluid and flexible against an enemy who was not. At least flexible by the usual USAAF standards.

Being attached directly to 5th AF Advon Headquarters, John naturally had ample opportunity to photograph some of the brass, mostly General Whitehead of course. The 5th AF Photo Lab catered directly to his command.

(Below) *A candid shot of General Ennis Whitehead, the hard hitting Kansan, at his desk in Port Moresby. This was one of a series of photos John shot of Whitehead working in his office. Whitehead was a real enlisted man's General. While in Tacloban in the Philippines a Colonel was trying to cut in on the chow line (of mostly enlisted men) and the mess cook kept batting away his plate, refusing to serve him. Annoyed, the Colonel finally asked, "When do the officers get served?" and the cook replied "After the General". "When's that?" the Colonel inquired and the cook replied, "After him." and point to the end of the line, where General Whitehead was standing (out of uniform) with his mess kit.* (John Stava Collection)

(Opposite) *1) General MacArthur puffing a cigar rather than his trademark corncob pipe - in truth MacArthur preferred cigars in private. 2) Top Brass from Washington: in the front from L-R: Chief of Staff General George C. Marshall, General Thomas Handy and General Walter Krueger, probably taken on December 13th, 1943 at Port Moresby. In less than two years General Handy would issue orders to MacArthur for the delivery of the first Atomic Bomb to it's final destination - Hiroshima. In the background is General Whitehead trying to catch up. General Marshall was the highest ranking member of the U.S. Army. 3) Another shot of General MacArthur and General Kenney taken December 12th 1944 from the ceremony at Luzon where Major Bong was awarded the C.M.H.. Colonel Hutchison, John's old commanding officer, is standing to MacArthur's left. 4) General Whitehead has a laugh with General Kenney during a visit of Under Secretary of War Robert Patterson. Underrated by history, Whitehead was a brilliant tactician and had the tenacity of a bulldog in his mission to defeat the Japanese. He drove his staff hard and was constantly scheming up new ways to defeat his foe - Kenney couldn't have had a better deputy commander. 5). A rare photo of General Whitehead in full dress uniform, possibly taken at his appointment to command of the 5th Air Force on June 15th of 1944 after Kenney was promoted to command the newly formed "Far East Air Forces" which merged the 5th and 13th Air Forces. 6) Kenney and Whitehead share a lighter moment at 5th AF Headquarters. Garrett Middlebrook recalled meeting up with Kenney at a reunion 15 years later "He had a gravely voice...he was a stocky little fella - man I'd hate to go up against him, he was stocky but he was short and he had that deep voice...they said he stood up to MacArthur real good". He certainly did and MacArthur respected him for it.* (Photos 1,2, 5: John Stava Collection, Photos 3, 6: National Archives, Photo #4 courtesy of Marc Wiederwax)

1.

2.

6.

3.

5.

4.

Sydney Leave 1944

Leave in Sydney Australia was the one chief perks 5th AF personnel could look forward to for some much needed R&R. Typically a group of men from the same unit would share the cost of a house or apartment, which was usually reserved by the group or squadron.

In the case of the 499th Squadron, 345th BG, the officers pooled funds and bought a posh four bedroom house on Rose Bay, which included a permanent taxi driver, George, whom they supplied with 100-octane aviation fuel and whom also knew where the best Aussie beer was sold, how to get drunken pilots back and forth to the Roosevelt Club and where to find the most luscious girls. Vic Tatelman recalled; "*After the horror and filth of New Guinea, what change of mood and attitude did that place bring. If New Guinea was hell, Sydney was heaven! Clean clothes, all the hot water showers one wanted, comfortable beds with an eager and willing bed partner; to this day the look back, the remembrances, the wonderful recalls, that warm glow returns.*"

Since much of the young Australian male population had been drained out of the country since they'd joined the war with Britain in 1939, for a bunch of young and eager American males showing up with plenty of cash to burn it was open season. Particularly with young and aggressive Australian women who hadn't had any young men around in three or four years.

Carl Camp fell for an Aussie woman named Patricia on one of his leaves whom he penned a lengthy poem in which he wrote:

> *She said, "You don't need bloody grog,*
> *To keep you in a week long fog,*
> *Mate all you bloody need is little old me!*
> *You've had too much of bloody hate,*
> *And bloody fear of death of late,*
> *I'll bloody cure all that, you wait and see!"*

Not all was fun and games and there was a rough and rowdy side to leave in Sydney reminiscent of the wild west. George Robinson of the 17th Recon recalls meeting up Bud Kilgore's nephew whom he described as a "crazy S.O.B." Kilgore's nephew challenged another B25 Pilot that he could fly twenty feet lower - a bet which he won, after landing with the top of a pecan tree in his fuselage. He also snuck them into an officers club with borrowed Colonel's "Bars" and decided to liven things up by starting a brawl at which point Robinson and a Captain cleared out and jumped into a taxi cab. The cab driver pulled a loaded .45 and told them "*My orders are to never leave when there's trouble. You can wait here or get the hell out*" at which point they ran off.

The nickname the Americans had for the Australian ladies was "Sheila's". They were by and large young single women looking for some action. With most the Australian men off fighting the war in North Africa and New Guinea, the Americans flowing in enjoyed an almost unbelievable wave of popularity. 43rd BG Pilot Harry Young asked an Australian Brigadier at the bar of the Australia Hotel '*How do you like our American Army of Occupation?*" to which the Australian replied: "*You mean bloody army of seduction, don't you?*"

A tame bunch by comparison, the 5th F Photo Lab team got their shot at the action in Sydney during the summer of 1944. Aside from a day hanging out at Bondi Beach, and another at the Sydney Zoo, they pretty much went their separate ways in search of a little adventure and didn't meet up again until it was time to head back to the war. From these photos it's clear John had a few interesting adventures of his own.

(Above) *Ed Fairchild of Niagara Falls, New York, "Jimmy", Fred Miller of Havre, Montana and Lee Riedel of Los Alamos, New Mexico hanging on the rocks at Bondi beach.*

(Below middle) *A "Sheila" John hooked up with a Bondi beach and her furry friend.* (John Stava Collection)

(Below bottom) *John with a couple of new friends. The caption on the back reads "Terry Collins and Sally O'Keefe -Wow-."* (John Stava Collection)

(Opposite top) *Bondi Beach, 'the' beach to go to in Sydney.* (John Stava Collection)

(Opposite bottom) *The Corner of Pitt Street and Park in Sydney, with the Criterion Hotel on the left. Built in 1874 The Criterion was one of the popular watering holes with it's three bars and is still there today in Sydney's Central Business district.* (John Stava Collection)

HOTEL
French Pastry
FRENCH COFFEE
MR BASIL

1.

2.

5.

3.

(This page, clockwise from upper left) 1) *John and friend at a dance, possibly one too many drinks at the Australia Bar, a popular hangout for 5th AF crewmen. Les Meyers, a tail gunner John served with in the 17th Recon, had this to say about his own leave in Sydney: "We went down to Sydney Australia on rest leave…the women wouldn't go out with the officers…don't know why, but I guess they didn't believe in them. I don't know. But I know I saw some officers wearing Sergeant Stripes…..hehe." 2) One sure way to tick off your commanding officer and the local officials was to fly under the Sydney Bridge, a favorite antic of hotshot pilots. 3) Parade, near the Prince Edward Hotel 4) Bathurst Station on the Green Line, circa 1944 5) The Anzac Memorial at Hyde Park, also called "The Shrine of Remembrance".* (John Stava Collection)

(Opposite page, clockwise from upper left) 1) *Smelling the flowers - a Koala at the Sydney Zoo. 2) I always have room for a snack! - a precarious shot of the lions at the Sydney Zoo. 3) View down Market Street in Sydney. Note the Sydney Cenotaph mid-way down the street, a WWI Memorial to sailors and soldiers which appears as the last photograph in this book.* (John Stava Collection)

4.

1.

2.

3.

5th AF Nose Art

No book on any Air Force circa WWII would be worth it's salt if it didn't include at least a sampling of the imaginative nose art and names that adorned nearly all the aircraft. As to be expected, most the names had a story or personal reference behind them. One of the more interesting ones was Vic Tatelman's B-25 "Dirty Dora", and how he discovered the origin of the name while on leave in Sydney. In his own words: *"On one such leave, I met a 38th Bomb Group pilot who knew the story of the naming of the airplane. One of the crew had met an Australian girl, Dora, who moved in with him for the week he was there. He was amazed and delighted at the talent (and virtuosity) of his young partner in bed; particularly at the height of her pleasure when she would inexplicably scream out the most profane obscenities, words that even shocked him, coming from a seemingly otherwise modest and sweet young girl. So the perfect name for the airplane, DIRTY DORA."*

"On a subsequent Sydney leave, I met Dora and explained that she was the namesake of my airplane, I even took her out to the airport to show her the name painted on the nose of the airplane; she was unimpressed!"

Although the quality of the artwork wasn't nearly has high as it typically was in the European theater, the names and histories on these aircraft was no less colorful. Included here are a sampling of the 40+ nose art images in John's collection.

(Left Top to Bottom) 1.) *Lewd Lady was a "war weary" 22nd BG B-25 Mitchell that was used as a courier plane or air taxi for the 5th Air Force. The caption on the back written by John Stava reads:* "Practically all our planes have names and pictures painted on the nose. Nude girls predominate - of course. Here is the illustration on the plane in which I do much of my flying - and a good lady she is!" 2.) *Montana Maid was a 17th Recon B-25 John flew on as a tail gunner on a series of hazardous missions in late 1944 with Harold Hilderman as pilot. Hilderman said he flew this B-25 on only four missions and then it went down with another crew.* 3 & 4.) *"Fat Cat" was a 3rd BG B25 the group "decomissioned" from combat and "Steak and Eggs" a 3rd BG A20 ground crews built from spare parts, the idea being to have an "off the books" aircraft the squadrons would keep for private use, that use being "milk runs" down to Australia to pick up extras for the Squadron such as Whiskey, fresh meat and vegetables, phonograph records, etc. The name "Steak and Eggs" tells the story quite obviously - fresh steak and eggs from Australia being a prized commodity of airmen in New Guinea usually subsisting on cans of "Bully beef" and powdered eggs. The story of Steak and Eggs is a saga all of it's own. She was a Frankenstein plane built from two aircraft - the fuselage was from "Little Hellion" which had bellied in at Port Moresby on Nov 1st 1942 and the wings were from another plane "Yellow Fever". She was constructed by 89th Squadron ground crews during down time while their regular aircraft were out on missions. She was completed on February 3rd 1943 and was christened by the Squadron Mess officer, Lt. Ocal P. Jones, with appropriately enough, a raw egg.. Labeled a "Flying mess kit" by an A.P. reporter, she made regular runs until crashing on a remote island called "Low Woody" by pilot Lt. Rude Vucelic after running out of fuel in late 1943. No-one was hurt but "Steak and Eggs" chow run days were over.* (John Stava Collection)

1.

2.

3.

4.

1.

2.

6.

3.

5.

4.

(Clockwise from upper left) 1) *"Pannell Job" was a B-25 flown by Lieutenant Ray Pannell of the 345th BG, 500th BS. He was killed when this plane went into a mysterious dive from 5,000 ft and crashed during a training mission on June 11th 1944 over Nadzab* 2) *"Heavenly Body" was a 380th BG 528th BS B-24 that is also listed as a 90th BG 400th BS plane - it may have been transferred.* 3) *A 90th BG B-24.* 4) *"Shag-on" was formerly a 312th BG A-20 that wound up with the 8th Service Group - a combat training unit out of Nadzab. She crashed on February 9th 1945 while on a strafing run on Muschu Island, killing her crew.* 5) *"Wolf Pack" was a B-24 that served with the 43rd BG and 22nd BG - she was shot down in January 1944 by Japanese fighters.* 6) *"Pam 3d" - no info is available on this P-38.* (John Stava Collection)

1.

2.

6.

3.

5.

4.

(Clockwise from upper left) 1) *"Island Queen" - a 22nd BG B-24 that went missing on June 9th 1944. She became separated from the formation by rainstorms 2 hours from the target which was Peleliu. Like so many planes, she simply vanished into the vast Pacific and was never heard of again.* 2) *"Bourbon Boxcar" was a F-7 from the 20th Combat Mapping Squadron, 6th Photo Mapping Group deployed out of Nadzab. The F-7 was the Recon version of the B-24. All of the 20th's creative nose art was painted by Al Merkling, a crack sketch artist from Philadelphia. Painting nose-art in the South Pacific was a real challange where the hot temperatures would bake the paint almost as quickly as it was applied.* 3) *"Wango Wango Bird" was also a F-7 Liberator of the 20th Combat Mapping Squadron. She met her end in April of 1944 when she stalled taking off from Nadzab. No-one was hurt although three Lightning pilots that had hitched a ride got a good scare, and were heard to comment afterwards that they would stick to flying fighters in the future.* 4) *"Cherokee Princess" was a 345th BG, 498th BS B-25. The artwork was painted by Sgt. Charles Pushetonequa, a Native American Indian from Tama, Iowa. Sgt. Pushetonequa was also responsible for coming up with the group insignia for the "Air Apaches", as the 345th Bomber Group elected to call itself from July of 1944 onwards.* 5) *"Snafu Maru", a 475th Fighter Group (Satan's Angels) P-38 from the 432nd Fighter Squadron flown by Captain Howard Hendrick.* 6) *The tail rudder of "Queen of Hearts" a B-24 from the 320th BS, showing the infamous "Skull and Cross Bombs" insignia of the 90th Bomber Group. Probably taken in the Philipppines.*(John Stava Collection)

1.

2.

3.

4.

5.

(Clockwise from upper left) 1) *"Mitch The Witch" was the grand old dame of the 17th Recon, shown here with an unknown crewman on the marston matting at Lingayen, Philippines. A replica B-25 of the Witch still flies on the air show circuit today.* 2) *"The Wolf Pack" was a 345th BG 501st Squadron B-25 that flew over 100 missions. She was lost on a transport mission between Biak and Nadzab on September 11th 1944 and force landed near the village of Angisi near Wewak after both engines went, however all 2 crew and 8 passengers made it to safety, assisted by natives. The co-pilot, F/O Beardsley, gave this account of the crash: ""the B-25 slashed through the swamp grasses like a big sickle. Landing with wheels up, it banged into the slimy muck and then slid like a toboggan for nearly 80 yards before jerking abruptly to a rest. A wisp of gray smoke swept across the windshield and the smoldering engines sizzled, but when they did not explode - when we all realized that were still alive - we were amazed." Her last mission was flying dirty laundry back to Nadzab.* 3) *"Redhot Ridinhood" was a B-24 of the 22nd Bomber Group.* 4) *"Old Man" - this B-17 #124403 was General Whithead's personal plane.* 5) *"Dirty Dora" - Vic Tatelman's infamous B-25, which was originally asigned to the 38th Bomber Group.* (Photo #1: Courtesy of Lester Meyers, Photos 2 & 3: John Stava Collection, Photo #4: Jerome Schrenk Collection, Photo #5: courtesy of Vic Tatelman)

Film Stock

These stills are from some of the rare 16mm color film reels John Stava shot in New Guinea. Below are stills from a flight of 22nd Bomber Group B-24s, with the reefs outside of Port Moresby clearly visible in the lower shot. One of the marvels of this current age is that I can go online, pull up "Google Earth" and within seconds be looking a virtual satellite image of these same reefs today, from the same angle and altitude. On the right column, "Sticky Kitty" was a 17th Recon B-25 number 42-87280 flown by Lt. H. E. Rogers that crashed into Bunabun Harbor near Wewak on February 6, 1944. Note the early 17th Recon markings on the rudders and also the bulged waist gun position, which was a field modification on this early B-25 model. Additional twin .50 caliber gun packs have been installed on either side of the fuselage. It's not clear whether Lt. Rogers is the pilot seen in these photos.

(John Stava Collection)

Philippines 1944-45

By the summer of 1944 the race was well on between Admiral Nimitz and General MacArthur. Nimitz was advocating a direct thrust through the Central Pacific with the intent to take Formosa while MacArthur was hell-bent on retaking the Philippines, starting with Mindanao, up through Leyte and into Manila, bypassing Formosa and thrusting directly up into Japan's underbelly. Both strategies had their merit and for a time history hung in the balance while each commander lobbied for Washington's support. Ultimately it came about, no doubt as a result of MacArthur's indominatable will and ability to convince the Washington representatives in his favor, that the invasion plans for Formosa were scrapped in favor of MacArthurs plan. MacArthur would get his triumphant return to the Philippines.

September of 1944 saw the 5th and 13th Air Forces softening up southern Mindanao, with careful attention being paid to the Japanese bases around Davao, setting the stage for the Battle of the Leyte Gulf in October, which would cost the Japanese three battleships, four carrier, six heavy cruisers, four light cruisers and eleven destroyers. As a naval power Japan would be effectively knocked out of the war, but still had a costly trump card to play.

In late October while the American troops on Leyte were hanging on precariously to their foothold there, the Kamikaze attacks would begin.

Nothing had prepared the Americans for anything like it Max Ferguson, 345th, 499 BS BG Veteran and author of "Bat's Outa Hell Over Biak" describes in detail the ordeal of surviving a Kamikaze attack on a troop ship while waiting to disembark on Leyte "There were only two men alive on the rear of the ship. A man on the port side was sitting upright in the middle of several dead - his left arm and shoulder blade had been completely blown off, but there was no bleeding. The next time I looked he had fallen forward." On a larger scale the continual Kamikaze attacks took their psychological toll on the American's - watching suicide planes flying through carpets of intense AA fire and crashing themselves into troop ships who were sitting ducks in Leyte harbor was no laughing matter - but it no doubt sped up the delayed unloading process up considerably.

On Leyte the amount of aircraft being funneled into the limited main airfield space at Tacloban was causing a serious backup, compounded by incessant rain that bogged down everything in mud. General Whitehead said to General Kenney: "Mud is still mud no matter how much you push it around with a bulldozer". The situation became so critical that any aircraft not immediately serviceable were plowed off the strip and into the ocean. To make matters worse a major typhoon would strike the area on December 17th, sinking 3 destroyers off to the east in the Philippine Sea and wreaking havoc on the shipping in Leyte

Around this time John Stava would transition from the 5th AF Advon photo lab and into a full time combat position with the 17th Recon Squadron as a tail gunner. In December the 5th AF would surprise the Japanese by invading Mindoro as a prelude for taking Luzon. It was a precarious situation and the Japanese were throwing everything they had to defend their last line of defense in the Philippines. Just after Christmas of 1944 they would counter with a convoy sent to attack the American foothold there, and as fate would have it the 17th Recon would be the only available medium bomber squadron available to intercept, which they would over four days of costly attacks from December 26th through December 30th. John would continue to fly intermittent

Map Source: General Drafting Co, Inc.

missions with the 17th Recon - around 20 all total - with his last recorded combat mission on May 10th 1945.

In December the 17th Recon would move up to San Jose on Mindoro and from there to Lingayen on Luzon where MacArthur would stage his return with a three pronged attack on the Capital at Manila.

Despite the Japanese determination to hold Manila at all costs, they would concede defeat after a brutal 30 day bloodbath from February 3rd to March 3rd that would leave most of the city destroyed. It was said to have suffered the most damage of any Allied city during WWII, topping Moscow and Stalingrad. Although General Yamashita had pulled his Army forces to the outskirts of the city, a good part of that destruction would be from the Japanese Naval troops under Rear Admiral Iwabuchi Sanji as they razed, burned, dynamited the city, and slaughtered civilians en masse as they fought to a bitter end.

The spring of 1945 would see the 5th turn much of it's attention to shipping intercepts off the China and Korean coasts while continuing clean up operations in Northern Luzon. From there they would make the final thrust up through Ie Shima into Japan to play out the final scene of the war.

(Opposite page) *On November 10th 1944 thirty B-25's of the 38th Bomber Group caught up with a Japanese convoy pulling out of Ormoc Bay at Leyte and gave them a pounding. Lt Edwin Polanski led the fourth flight of the 822nd Squadron on this destroyer, taking some heavy AA damage on his attack run. They were hit by a series of explosions as they passed over the ship, which mortally wounded a photographer they had on board. Later when they landed a Doctor looked at the wounded man and pulled a blanket over his face before the crew got a chance to ask how he was. The 822nd would lose five of their 8 planes on this mission but the Japanese would pay with two of their precious cargo vessels. This destroyer has just taken a serious direct hit amidships.* (Robert Stava Collection)

The 17th Recon: Tacloban

In November of 1944 on the heels of the battle for the Leyte Gulf the 17th Reconnaissance would arrive at Tacloban in the Philippines which as fate would have it, coincided with the rainy season. The site had been captured in October and engineers had thrown together an airstrip in only two days on a sand peninsula jutting out into the ocean. The strip itself was made of pierced steel planking (also called 'Marston' matting) that received so much aircraft traffic that it actually crawled across the sand several inches per day. If you were taking off with a full bomb load you could actually see a ripple in the matting ahead of the plane.

The situation at Tacloban was chaotic - backed up shipping in the Leyte gulf were sitting ducks for Kamikaze attacks and the Japanese made several aggressive airstrikes at the cramped facilities there.

Most crew were bivouacked in tents to the south of the strip and was jammed to capacity. The road that led down to the small village of Tacloban was lined with trucks and jeeps, although the 17th personnel wound up on a hill near the airstrip. One night a bizarre incident occurred when a Japanese troop transport appeared over the harbor area, drawing anti-aircraft fire from all the ships as well as from the airstrip and amazingly managed to make it all the way to a crash landing right on the runway. It wasn't clear just what they'd hoped to accomplish but the plane was loaded with 15 marines in full battle gear - half who were killed in the crash and the rest were shot or captured as they crawled out of the wreckage. George "Red" Robinson recalled *"It was crazy. Well, two things. Here comes a colonel. He wants everyone to come down. They took over our airfield* (Author: at least tried). *We hadn't been able to fly it anyway. So they got this group to go in on the ground and retake the airfield. They asked for volunteers, and like a damned fool I volunteered. So the first four, they give us all machine guns. And they said 'everybody else, just fall in behind whoever you want to.' Well I got a good gang. And about that time, a jeep turned in... muddy all over, and a fella got out, no rank, no nothing on his uniform. It was General Whitehead! And brother he tore that Colonel up. He said 'You're not going to send these guys - these are not ground troops, these are well trained flying personnel and they're going to fly, and they're not going in on the ground.' So he stopped it and we didn't have to go."*

George also recalled how they hired a Filipino boy to run errands around their tent and to get them local provisions: *"They'd walk up a palm tree with a machete, and they'd knock down a green coconut, we'd cut the top off of it and drink it. That's where we had our fresh water. He told me he'd get me some bananas, so we went out to get some bananas and boy we found 'em. I had bananas hanging up all around my tent. Anyway I had one load of bananas on my shoulder and he said, (in a falsetto voice) 'Excuse me sir, there's a spider and he will kill you!' So I set it down and sure enough there was one of those deadly spiders there and I said, "Aw, he won't hurt you, he's too little." And the boy said 'Well, he kill a Filipino, but he make an American sick I bet!'"*

The 17th Recon would stay at Tacloban barely a month before packing up to a forward base at San Jose in Mindoro which would shortly become even more perilous than Tacloban.

(Below) *The mud on Leyte was legendary, swallowing up entire vehicles if you believe the stories. The caption on the photo lower left reads "'Just to show you the mud we slop around in during this rainy season." and lower right "More mud - typical bamboo and palm frond shacks" Les Meyers: "Mud. That was always a problem". You get the idea.* (John Stava Collection)

(Opposite Page Top) *Main Street in Tacloban.* (John Stava Collection)

(Opposite Page Bottom) *One business that sprang right into action with the arrival of the Americans was the Filipino laundry. This photo shows the Tacloban branch in operation. Getting your pants washed would set you back fifteen centavos and twenty centavos for a shirt, a centavo being roughly half an American cent. Filipinos also picked up work around the camp for 100 centavos per day, plus food and cigarettes. With the heavy influx of American servicemen into the area however those prices didn't last long as the old classic rules of supply and demand kicked in and prices skyrocketed.* (John Stava Collection)

3.

Philippine Life: Tacloban

After the sweating jungles of New Guinea and the stark barrenness of Biak the Philippines must have seemed like a major step towards civilization for the 5th AF crewmen. During the Japanese occupation life had been brutal on the Filipinos with large amounts of the rural population moving out of the villages and up into the mountains to either join the guerrilla army or simply escape the Japanese occupiers. Some took to simply killing the occasional Japanese soldier when they could and others gathered detail on Japanese troop movements and concentrations to pass onto the allies.

Looking at these scenes that suggest serenity in rural Philippine life it's difficult to concieve that barely two months previous Leyte was a vicious battleground as MacArthur staged his triumphant return to the Philippines here. By the time the U.S. forces arrived most of the Filippinos here were ragged and hungry from two and a half years of living under an oppresive occupying army and a black market of increasingly scarcer food and ever inflating prices.

Many of the 5th Servicemen would hire young Filippino boys as "house boys" - running odd errands, getting local food and such. All of the veterans I spoke with underlined how generous and self-sacrificing the Filippino's were to the American soldiers.

(Below) *There's something timeless and serene in this photo of a Filipino girl measuring corn into a shallow basket.* (John Stava Collection)

(Opposite Page) *Clockwise from upper left: caption on back says "Miss Leyte 1944", Filipino women shelling rice the old fashioned way, an elderly woman caught in a moment of retrospection, a thatch roofed house indicative of the rural lifestyle on Tacloban.* (John Stava Collection)

(Above) *The Provincial Capital Building on Leyte, or whats left of it. Apparently the previous tenants needed a little urging to vacate.* (John Stava Collection)

(Right) *A Caraboa cools off in the mud. On the back John wrote: "A very contented cariboa - better known to us as a water buffalo. Used as a beast of burden much as an ox."* (John Stava Collection)

(Opposite Page) *Another moment of domestic tranquility - a Filipino woman works a loom.* (John Stava Collection)

Strike Force at San Jose

In December the 17th Recon moved up to San Jose on Mindoro and would in short order get into some very hot action. On the evening of December 26th it was discovered that the Japanese had sent a naval task force consisting of a battleship, a heavy cruiser, and six destroyers to wipe out the newly established 5th AF base there. Only the 17th Recon was at hand to intercept the convoy along with 20 P-40s of the 110 Tactical Recon Squadron. The first night the squadron attacked twice until the convoy came within closing distance of the airfield and started shelling it, at which point the 17th Recon's B-25s were forced to fly back to Tacloban. Additionally Japanese fighters kept showing up and strafing the airfield, at one point hitting the ammo dump. Radio Operator George Robinson from Kilgore's crew recalled *"They'd come through strafing and we'd hit a foxhole. We'd start an engine run back to the foxhole, and finally we got everything started and we took off. We didn't know if we were going to be blown up on the runway or not. Yeah, that was kind of big."*

Events were chaotic with 17th Recon planes taking off and attacking the task force, which by this point was 15 miles NW of the base, in sporadic attacks. Lt. Kluth's crew took off at 7:30pm, sank a destroyer, landed, reloaded and was taking off again when their B-25 rammed a P-40 also taking off, they jumped into another plane and attacked the convoy again, sinking another ship. Hilderman's crew, with John flying tail gunner, missed out on the excitement - they initially missed the convoy, salvoed their bombs due to low fuel, then found the convoy but couldn't attack without bombs, then high tailed it back to Tacloban on Leyte. Fate would give them a chance to make up for the missed opportunity four days later.

The action would cost the 17th one B-25 wrecked on take off, two ditched en route back to Tacloban, one shot down over the convoy and one missing without a trace, most likely to low fuel and bad weather. Three air crew were dead, eleven were missing in action and fourteen were injured. One B-25 piloted by Lt. William Hatcher of Albany, Texas, was observed to have crashed his plane deliberately into a Japanese destroyer after being mortally hit by flak, sinking the ship. That was a shocking event in itself that none of the veteran's I interviewed would discuss. In turn of the enemy convoy the heavy cruiser was badly damaged, two destroyers were sunk, one seriously damaged, one transport ship was probably sunk along with a submarine.

For the 17th Recon crews, their troubles were hardly over. While the airfield was still being shelled by Japanese Naval fire, heavy storms set in and the decision was been made to temporaily abandon the airfield at San Juan and fly back to Tacloban. George Robinson recalled two paratroopers who were terrified at being left behind and jumped into Kilgore's plane just before they took off. Captain Sill's plane would be one of those who ran out of fuel and ditched - near the northern tip of Samar Island where he and his crew were fortunately picked up by Filipinos in canoes and taken to Tacloban. Lt. Burwell Vowell's disappeared between Mindoro and Leyte and was never seen or heard from again.

Kilgore's plane became lost and was running perilously low on fuel near Leyte, and no-one would answer their "mayday" distress call (apparently radio silence was effective due to the Japanese attackers). They were dumping everything overboard and preparing to ditch the plane when like a miracle the clouds parted and a single searchlight beam appeared, guiding them to the runway. As they landed the engines quit, completely out of fuel.

Due to the fact that the missions happened at night and the ensuing chaos of the airstrip being under attack, no known photographs of these missions exist.

Three days later on December 30th the 17th was back in the thick of it again, joining in on another attack off the west coast of Luzon on another enemy convoy of four troop transports, three destroyers and a cruiser. John would be flying tail gunner in a B-25 #992 piloted by Lt. Harold Hilderman that would take out one of the destroyers with a direct hit - it would lift the bow clear out of the water and cause the ship to explode. The convoy would take a mauling and end the attempt to repel the allies off Mindoro, and December 1944 would prove to be one of the most memorable in the squadrons history.

(Opposite page clockwise) 1) *Al Cottman (foreground) poses with his crew - from L-R: Lt. Earl Root (navigator), Lt. Bernard Foster, (co-pilot) and Lt. Bishop "Bud" Kilgore (pilot). Cottman was a tall, quiet man from Pennsylvania and a good friend of George Robinson - he once calmly talked Robinson into taking his tentmate Harold Ford (See page #118) back after a fight where Ford pulled a .45 and said "This tent aint big enough for both of us.". "Bud" Kilgore was described as a "gung-ho" pilot who was always up for something including a promotion. 2) Shot of John Stava at Mindoro with a couple of the 17th's mascots - the dog on the right is "Cosmo". 3) General Whitehead flies a B-25 in the co-pilot seat. The 17th Recon was General Whitehead's "pet squadron" and on a flight up to San Jose on December 22nd, 1944 Whitehead insisted on flying the plane. According to George Robinson who was on the flight:* "...they told him they couldn't land at Mindoro, he said "I got a pilot that'll land there and I'll go with him and see that he does. And so we flew up there. Of course we had fighter escort. So he (Whitehead) got a hold and started flying the plane. Over there and back. Because he was a pilot. And Kilgore would reach over with his left hand and pull the stick up - you know how the wheel is shaped - and he'd (Kilgore) pull it up when Whitehead would go down and when (Whitehead) started climbin' he'd reach over and push it down. If anybody asked him "Hell, I couldn't tell the General; he didn't know how to fly!" *Robinson went on to say:* "What I recall about General Whitehead was that he was a fair, honest gentleman. And he didn't put up with no bull." *After the war when Whitehead had retired and was living in Florida an article appeared in a paper where he invited "Anybody from the old outfit to come by and see him, any time." 4) Excerpt from John's citation report on the December 30th mission which earned him a fourh Oak Leaf CLuster - the equivilent of being awarded the Air Medal a fourth time. 5) The incorrigable and mischievous George "Red" Robinson from Port Arthur, Texas. George recalled that his pilot "Bud" Kilgore was a real by-the-book type and a straight shooter - he was one of the only pilots that kept the stiffeners in his pilot's cap (Which traditionally all Air Force pilots would take out), until George got a hold of his cap one day and "accidentally" stomped the hell out of it and dragged it around camp, giving it the respectably "rumpled" look he felt it deserved before returning it. Kilgore never said a word about it.* (All images John Stava Collection)

1.

2.

5.

3.

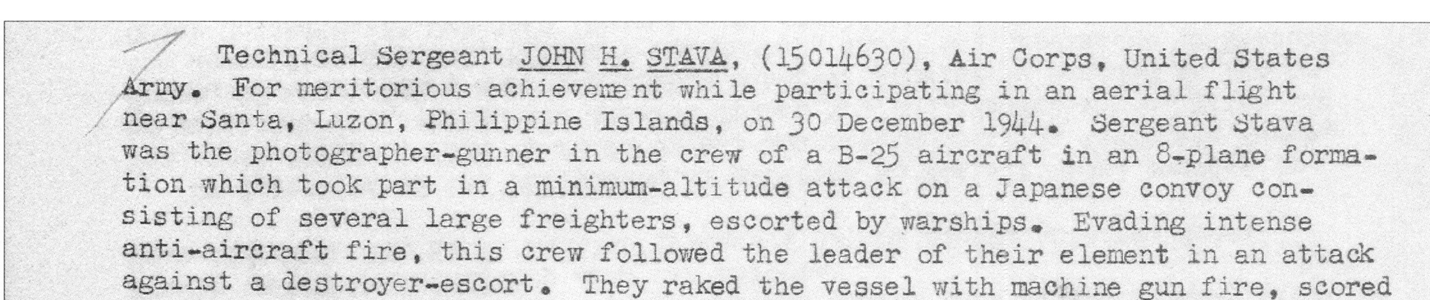

Technical Sergeant JOHN H. STAVA, (15014630), Air Corps, United States Army. For meritorious achievement while participating in an aerial flight near Santa, Luzon, Philippine Islands, on 30 December 1944. Sergeant Stava was the photographer-gunner in the crew of a B-25 aircraft in an 8-plane formation which took part in a minimum-altitude attack on a Japanese convoy consisting of several large freighters, escorted by warships. Evading intense anti-aircraft fire, this crew followed the leader of their element in an attack against a destroyer-escort. They raked the vessel with machine gun fire, scored two near misses, and dropped a third bomb which exploded directly beneath the

4.

(Above Left) *San Jose on Mindoro.* (John Stava Collection)

(Above Right) *A grinning Sgt. John Malone on Mindoro, unaware of what the fates have in store from him. As a turret gunner with Lt. Brown's crew, they were forced to ditch near Pacijan Island on the December 26th Mission after running out of fuel attempting to reach Tacloban, landing in rough seas at 130 mph. Lt. Brown and his co-pilot managed to get Malone and Cpl. Cavanaugh into the life raft, although Cavanaugh died shortly from a deep gash in his head. The navigator Lt. Herbert drowned trying to swim to shore but Cpl Bondie, despite two crushed legs, managed to swim 200 yards to shore. On March 6th after a strike against Hainan Island off the China coast, Lt Brown was again forced to ditch his B-25, this time off the south coast of Luzon, and this time the intrepid Sgt Malone made a dramatic rescue of the crew with the help of Navigator Lt. Mueller although the remaining two crew were mangled - the waist gunner had his leg completely severed - and sank with the plane. The life raft turned out to be punctured although Sgt. Malone somehow managed to keep it inflated until they were rescued by native Filipinos in outrigger canoes some 30 minutes after the crash. One wonders if Malone started thinking about crewing with another pilot after that.* (John Stava Collection)

(Below left) *Harok, Les Meyers, and George Carr with Gene Oterson and "Cosmo" in front. Les Meyers recalled the hazards of low level flying in the Philippines: "...one (B-25) plane came back, he came down so low he hit the top of a telephone pole. He came back with a piece of metal that had on there "Bethlehem Steel. I think that was in Manila"*
(Below Right) *17th Recon encampment on Mindoro.* (John Stava Collection)

(Opposite Page Top) *Goodrich's crew strike a pose in front of "Mitch The Witch" - an older D model B-25 still flying with the 17th Recon - at Lingayen. The 17th didn't move up to Lingayen until April 5th, so that would most likely date this photo as after that. Back row L-R: Lt. Willard Goodrich, Lt. M.V. Catlin, front row L-R Sgt. Lester Meyers, Cpl. Eugene Oterson, Sgt. George B. Carr. Lt. Goodrich was called "Pappy" by the crew as he was much older. Les Meyers gave many insights on life with the 17th Recon including contributing this photo. I found George Carr living in Staten Island although due to his health he was unable to contribute much, he did recall Lt. Goodrich and that he was from California. In another odd twist of coincidence, I discovered that one of John's regular crew, radio operator Norris Abbott, lived right down the street and was friends with my brother-in-laws family out in Westhampton Beach, although he'd unfortunately just passed away when I made the connection.* (Courtesy of Lester Meyers)

(Opposite Page Bottom) *Anonymous poem written by a 17th Recon personnel about the December 26th Mission.*

"Christmas Aftermath"
or "Gray Hairs in the Making"

T'was the night after Christmas,
And all through the island,
Not a person was joking,
And no-one was smilin'

The word got around
That a convoy was sighted,
So the Fighting 17th
Was called on to fight it.

The crews were lined up
and were briefed as to where
They would find the nip Task Force
That was sighted out there.

So they gathered their flak suits
And helmets and stuff,
For they knew that this mission
Was bound to be rough.

With shouts of "Good Luck"
They climbed into their ships
And started their engines
To go after the Nips.

Major Wise was the first
To get off the ground
For he knew the spot
Where the Nips would be found.

The rest of the boys
Took off one by one
Each saying a prayer
As he gave it the gun.

The battle that followed
Near the shores of Mindoro
Gave the Japs quite a headache
Not to mention much sorrow.

The light of the moon
Was lost in the glow
Of ack-ack and flames
That burst over the show

Each man at the wheel
Of his B-25
Put aside all his fears
As he started his dive

With wide open throttle
And open bomb bay
He roared o'er the target,
"The bombs are away!"

Explosions and fires
Flared up in the night
When Joe and his boys
Showed the Japs how to fight.

The Nips on their ships
Gave out with loud groans
As they sank 'neath the surface
To meet Davey Jones.

Yes, the night after Christmas
Is one that will stay
In the minds of us all
Who are living this day.

And we'll never foget,
The job that was done
By the lads who gave all
That the fight might be won.

America's Top Ace: Major Richard I. Bong

Except for mostly aviation buffs, it's sad to say that few people today know that Major Dick Bong was and still is America's highest scoring ace at 40 kills. A quiet, unassuming man from Poplar, Wisconsin, he hardly fit the typical archetype of the "Ace Fighter Pilot". He rarely smoked or drank and was socially uncomfortable with his fellow pilots. Garrett Middlebrook, a 38th BG B25 Pilot, struck up an acquaintance with him on a ship back to the states in late '43 and said "He did not articulate well nor as fast as some of the others; consequently, he seemed ill-at-ease in describing his experience when the little group of pilots were all present" Middlebrook gained Bong's confidence on the ride back - and it soon came to light that Bong had come to his aid one day by taking on and shooting down the "Black Predator" - a tenacious "Oscar" pilot that had dogged the 38th for many missions, although Bong was never officially credited with the kill.

"Marge" - Bong's sweetheart and later wife, came to adorn his plane with a blow up made from a wallet-size photo he carried with him always, which was provided by the the 5th AF Photo Section. Capt. Jim Nichols from Intelligence came up with the original idea of using Marge's graduation photo, the enlargement which he hand tinted and applied to Bong's plane with about twenty-five coats of varnish. According to Bob Crowe, Major Bong would "Drop by every month or so for a new print as he was either losing planes in combat or the photos were wearing off."

Sadly, Major Bong would die the same day as the Atomic Bomb was dropped, flying a P80 jet he was testing into a Los Angeles parking lot rather than risking civilian casualties by bailing out over a residential area. In the later 1990's I got in touch with Marge and sent her copies of these photos which she had never seen before and was delighted to have - I donated them to the Richard I Bong Heritage Center in Wisconsin. Marge finally passed away in 2003 after a long bout with cancer.

(Left) *A classic photo John Stava took of Major Bong as he sits in his cockpit of his infamous P38 "Marge" at Nadzab in Apri. of 1944.* (John Stava Collection)

(Above) *Another shot John Stava took on December 12th, 1944 on Leyte, Philippines, of Major Bong with General MacArthur and General Kenney when Major Bong was awarded the Congressional Medal of Honor at Tacloban Airfield. On the back of the photo it says; "Major Bong, "Dugout" Doug and General Kenney". I was curious how my uncle might have come about to take this photo until I found the photo lower right in the National Archives of the same event, with Colonel David W. Hutchison - John's former boss from the Photo Section - clowning around with Dick Bong and General Kenney.* (John Stava Collection)

(Below left) *A rather scruffy looking Bong in New Guinea. For a man of such amazing achievements it's remarkable and sad how many of his peers treated him with such disrespect. Marge recalled some (Stateside) trainees were even so bold as to approach him at a restaurant and openly question his kill record. Garrett Middlebrook also recalled how he took the brunt of many taunts and jokes on his first trip back in 1943.* (National Archives)

Clark Field: January 7th

The morning of January 7th saw the first concentrated low level attack against Clark Field since 1942. 40 B-25's of the 345th BG were joined by 36 A-20's of the 312th & BG along with two squadrons of P-38's as well as A-20's of the 417th BG in an effort to eliminate Clark as a major Japanese Airfield on Luzon. Clark Field was located Northwest of Manila and one of the major sources of Kamikaze squadrons plaguing the American invasion fleet steaming towards the Lingayen gulf, which the attackers passed over en route to the target near Mindoro.

Things were looking well for the attacking force - which had flown up from Tacloban - until they closed on the target. Low lying clouds broke up the formations and things started to get a little hairy as 132 aircraft jinked through the overcast. In one instance Sgt. Ira Schaub, a turret gunner with the 498th Squadron, spent a few tense seconds nervously eyeing a propeller spinning four feet above his head. Finally the attackers broke through the weather and spread out as they prepared to sweep the air base. The fun and games were just beginning. The faster A-20's crossed paths with the 345th, dropping parafrag bombs in strings that some of the 345th B-25s had to fly through. In the chaos of criss-crossing aircraft some A-20's actually formed up with B-25s while other B-25's dropped right down on the deck to avoid collision. Such was the case with Captain Floyd Fox who raced his B-25 ten feet off the ground on his attack run - so low the prop wash was parting the kunai grass. Additionally around a half dozen Japanese fighters circling overhead dropped phospherous bombs onto the attacking formations but their timing was off and the bombs wound up exploding behind the attacking wave and only added to the destruction on the ground.

Despite all this the attack was a success, if only for the fact that afterwards there were only a few sporadic kamikaze attacks and the massive invasion convoy that landed January 9th at Lingayen suffered only minor damage. It wasn't until after the American ground forces reached Clark Field that they discovered that nearly 1500 Japanese aircraft had been knocked out of action on the ground since the 5th Air Force raids had started the previous October. Strangely, many of the abandoned aircraft needed only a few basic spare parts to fly - the Japanese had attempted to disperse their shops and supplies as an answer to Allied raids, but only wound up tying themselves up in knots.

(Left) *Parafrags from Lt. McKinney's B-25 of the 498th BS, 345th BG, drift down over a dispersal area at Clark Field, 10:30 in the morning of January 7th, 1945. A Mitsubishi G4M "Betty" is in the lower right, A Ki-49 "Helen" to the far left, with some derilect Ki 48 "Lily's" and Ki45 "Nicks" in the background.* (Courtesy of Vic Tatelman)

(Above) *Passing over the main hangar complex at Clark Field, this photo was taken from the rear camera of Lt. John Cooper's B-25, also from the 498th squadron. In the background you can clearly see one of the phospherous bombs exploding - dropped by one of the circling Japanese fighters. 49?th Squadron pilot Vic Tatelman, didn't have have much good to say about the mission: "The Jan. 7 mission to Clark was hairy; my element was suddenly in a gaggle with a bunch of A-20s that apparently came out of nowhere.". Considering the amount of chaos ensuing over the target, it's a wonder there weren't any plane to plane collisions. Four A-20's from the 312th were lost from AA and one B-25 from the 345th BG - Sag Harbor Express, who after pulling up to avoid an A-20 was hit by AA fire, struggled along until it clipped a church steeple in nearby Angeles which tore off one wing, subsequently crashing and killing the entire crew.* (Courtesy of Vic Tatelman)

(Right) *Later January saw the 5th giving some attention to Japanese ground installations in and around the Bataan Peninsula. This shot was taken on January 24th, 1945, during an attack on Grande Island, showing the Japanese barracks there burning fiercely.* (Courtesy of Vic Tatelman)

The Propaganda War

Every war has it's propaganda and of course the war in the Southwest Pacific was no exception. While some propaganda wandered into the realm of overactive imaginations - like the myth of "Tokyo Rose", the supposed seductive female Japanese radio announcer who taunted American Servicemen with tales of recently captured soldiers or casualties (in fact, there was never a Japanese announcer who identified themselves as such, although there were several Japanese women who broadcasted programs) - there were still no shortage of very real attempts to brainwash the opposition.

Both sides would drop loads of leaflets from aircraft flying over enemy positions, urging them to give up, reminding them of the futility of fighting, recommending surrender as the only sane course of action, suggesting that their loved ones at home were hell-bent on being unfaithful. The 17th Recon flew at least a few of these "Propaganda missions". While it's doubtful these attempts had much of an impact on the war one way or another, included here are a sample of the type of leaflets that would be dropped over the Philippines.

(Below Left) *This leaflet is pretty self-explanatory, basically guaranteeing fair treatment in accordance with international law for any Japanese who surrender with this pamphlet. The photo shows similar soldiers who have already "been with us" and are being treated well. Note the word "Surrender" isn't actually used, as that was be considered shameful by the Japanese.* (Courtesy of George Robinson)

(Below Right) *This pamphlet was distributed after the war had ended and was geared towards holdouts who weren't convinced. The cover indicates : "The war has ended, peace has come. Soldiers will leave war zone and will be home soon."* (Courtesy of George Robinson)

(Opposite Page) *This somewhat unusual item is a children's booklet that would have been taught in schools of areas under Japanese occupation, in this case the Philippines. The title reads (roughly) "Far East United Front Proclamation". This was the "surface" PR rationale the Japanese used for taking over all of Asia - that all Asian peoples needed to be united against the evil Westerners who were corrupting them. The booklet explains in children's terms - with somewhat sinister undertones - how strong Asia will become under this new (Japanese led) rule and of course suggests that the best language everyone should speak is....Japanese. This booklet was presented to George Robinson by the mayor of Tacloban shortly after their arrival as a keepsake. No doubt the Mayor had no desire to hang onto it.* (Courtesy of George Robinson)

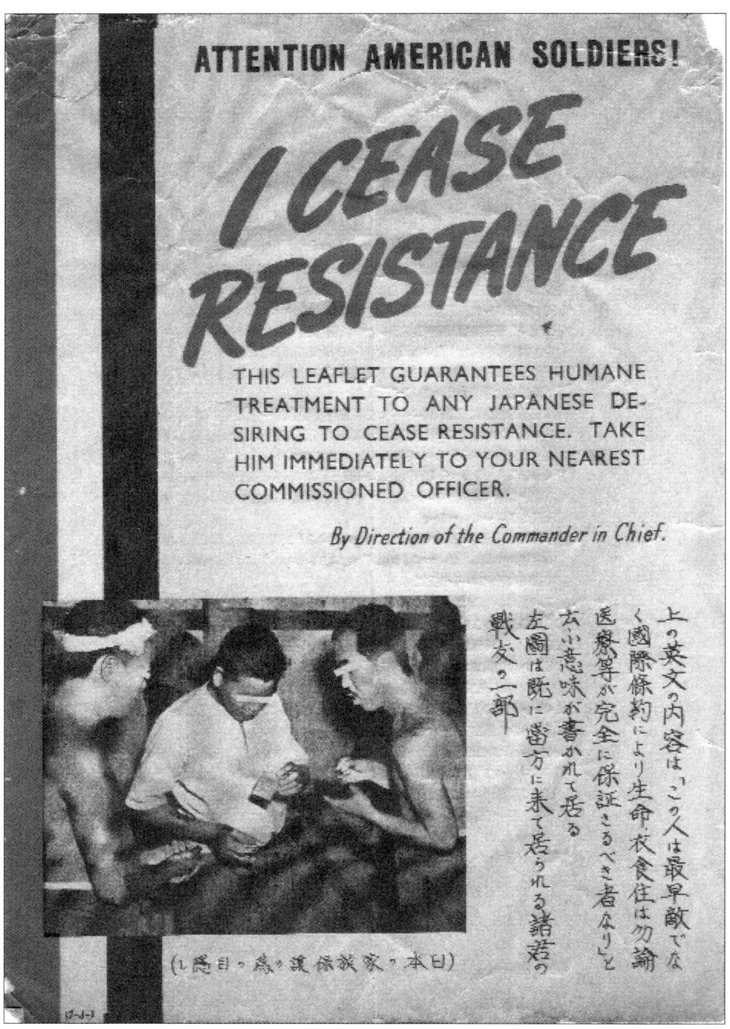

ダイトウアキョウドウセンゲン
大日本雄辯會講談社

A Day in Manilla

The battle for Manila occurred from February 3rd 1945 to March 9th, and had the dubious distinction of being the most devestated Allied city of WWII. Within that month-long bloodbath over 100,000 Filipino civilians would perish along with16,000 Japanese soldiers and around 1,000 Americans. Thus the "everydayness" of these photos is striking in their context. Less than two months previous to these photos being taken the city was still occupied by Japanese Naval troops that were hell bent on destroying the city population and razing everything around them as they fought to the death. And yet here are the city's populace going about the normal routines of daily life - selling goods at the market, washing clothes, going to work.

Ken Barber, a B25 pilot with the 17th Recon, had this recollection of leave in Manila: "The first was in early April 1945 when we were picked up at one of the local airports by a young Filipino man, a graduate of NYU whose family had contracted with the aircorps to provide rest leave for us in there half completed mansion is the Quezon City area north of Manila. It was a suburb somewhat like the Beverly Hills of California, although not that palatial. They arranged a party in a private home where we got to dance with some of the local girls. One in particular I still remember, she was a real beauty. Her parents were a Castilian Spanish lady and a wealthy Chinese merchant. She was only 19 at the time. They had a very strict chaperone code- NO TOUCH. We did not venture into the city of Manila other than to pass through it as we were driving to and from Quezon City. We were told that if we did, we had to be at least in pairs and armed."

(Left) *A woman shrewdly guards her wares - baskets of chickens and dried fish.* (John Stava Collection)

(Right) *Quiapo Church in Manila - it was restored in the 1980's after an earthquake but still looks pretty much the same today.* (John Stava Collection)

(Below) *Manila laid waste.* (John Stava Collection)

(Top and Right) *Chinese Cemetery in Manila, located in a suburb of Santa Cruz. An eerie place - it is a town for the dead complete with streets and tombs built as houses, many of them with furniture, running water and even air conditioning. Every Sunday the Chinese come to honor their dead lavish feasts are arranged and relatives sit around at the table playing Mahjong games, with an empty chair left for the departed.* (John Stava Collection)

(Above) *Another shot of the market in Manilla.* (John Stava Collection)

1.

2.

3.

6.

(Clockwise from upper left) *1) Rizal Monument in Rizal Park, Manila, named after Jose Rizal who was executed by the Spanish in 1896 2) Manila Hotel 3) Sports Arena, made of stainless steel and looking like someone took a flame-thrower to it. 4) Stainless Steel Church. 5) Sailors sauntering down an unknown block - safety in numbers was a good rule of thumb. 6) City Hall, looking like both armies used it for target practice.* (John Stava Collection)

5.

4.

(Above) *Apparently there are some things even bitter enemies can agree are sacred - beer being one of them. In stark contrast to the shelled and blasted buildings everywhere, the San Miguel Brewery in Manila stands spotless and unmarked. John wrote on the back of this photo "Not a scratch on it!"* (John Stava Collection)

(Below L- R) *1) As these photos from 22nd BG veteran Jerome Schrenk clearly indicate, the San Miguel brewery was very much open for business right away. That's Sgt. Schrenk in the far left photo filling a keg with beer.* (Jerome Schrenk Collection)

Convoy Hunt, March 30th, 1945, South China Sea

Early on the morning of March 29th about 60 miles off the east coast of Annam, French Indochina, B-25s of the 345th Bomber Group managed to finally find a convoy they'd previously hit on March 29th - five frigates, one freighter and a crippled destroyer. With such heavy AA defenses from the escorts this would definitely prove to be a rough target. Then, according to Lawrence Hickey's version in "Warpath Across the Pacific", things went awry. An American submarine torpedoed one of the frigates, sinking it. Two of the frigates broke off to rescue survivors while the other four ships high-tailed it towards a heavy weather system, hoping to shake the attackers in the rain squalls. The 498th and 501st Squadrons zeroed in on the two frigates and sealed their fates. The first ship had steel plates blasted off it's starboard side by the nose guns of Lt. Manners B-25 which went sailing 40 or 50 feet up into the air, then a series of 500lb bombs were skipped into it bow and midships. Within 30 minutes it was abandoned by it's crew and burning, rolled over and sank. The second frigate didn't last much longer - it was straddled by bombs repeatedly until a huge hole opened up in her flank and she sank quickly.

Meanwhile the remaining Air Apaches chased the rest of the convoy into squall systems where things got "quite spooky" with ships appearing and disappearing out of the mists and squalls and the risk of mid-air collisions running high. Even so one of the frigates and the freighter/tanker were almost certainly sunk. Amazingly in all the attacks only one 345th crewman was wounded - a slight bullet graze.

(Opposite page) *Frigate at the rear of the convoy getting blitzed by the Air Apaches. One of the mysteries surrounding this mission and the subsequent April 6th one on the following pages is whether John was in fact flying with the 345th BG as a tail gunner, as his notes on the photos in his collection would indicate. All the available evidence indicates it was certainly possible. At the time of these missions the 17th Recon was transitioning from San Jose to Lingayen and wasn't flying combat missions, Les Meyers commented 'He could have flown with that squadron, since he wasn't strictly assigned…not one of our permanent personnel so he could have been switching around." John would have been well connected with his lengthy service as a combat photographer under General Whitehead and at the time both the 345th BG and 17th Recon were operating in the same vicinity. Unfortunately no flight rosters of these missions remain - they are one of the squadrons that the National Archives doesn't have this information on and Larry Hickeys research staff, probably the De Facto experts on the 345th BG, came up empty handed as well, as did official 345th BG historian Paul Van Valkenburg. My own conclusion was that he wrangled his way into these missions as a tail-gunner, possibly as a last minute replacement.* (John Stava Collection)

(Above) *The second frigate at the rear of the convoy making a futile effort to survive, caught just as a 501st Squadron B-25 has released it's bombs. Dead and injured litter the decks while some crew can be seen cringing for cover.* (John Stava Collection)

(Right) *This photo in John's collection is perhaps another clue, the placard of the 500th BS "Rough Raiders". This photo was probably taken at Biak.* (John Stava Collection)

Destroyer Hunt, April 6th, 1945, South China Sea

B-25's from the 345th Bomber Group located two Kaibokan Class Frigates near the island of Quemoy off the China Coast just after 11:30 in the morning of April 6th. The first frigate was hit by six B-25s of the 501st Squadron and was sunk in a matter of minutes. The 501st then turned their attention to the second frigate and scored one direct hit and a few near misses but it was the B-25's of the 499th Squadron that finished her sentence, although she continued to bite until the end - Anti-Aircraft guns holed several B-25's and even knocked out one engine on Lt. Charles Myers, Jr's plane just before she rolled over and sank. The 498th Squadron arrived only to find two sinking ships and the water littered with Japanese sailors.

(Below) *This shot was taken from the fixed camera at the back of the B25, with John Stava's notes written on the original print. My best guess is that John was the tail gunner on Capt George Musket's aircraft as he was the first to score a direct hit on this ship and the lack of fire and smoke indicates this photo was probably that first direct hit.* (John Stava Collection)

(Opposite Top) *This dramatic shot captures the fatal explosion from a bomb delivered by Lt. Lester Morton's plane, which caused the ship to roll over within minutes.* (John Stava Collection)

(Opposite bottom) *Dubbed "The Air Picture of the Year" by the 345th BG which the Army Air Force's intelligence magazine IMPACT concurred in their June, 1945 release, this photo shows the doomed 80 odd Japanese crewmen clinging precariously to the hull and floating in the water. Their respite from death was short-lived - they were soon to become prey to the 498th Squadrons subsequent strafing passes. This photo was taken by the automatic tail camera on Capt. Frederick F. Smith's B-25 as he passed over the target and became one of the more famous photos to come out of WWII.* (John Stava Collection)

Close Call over Hainan

On March 6th 1945 Lt. Goodrich and his crew were about to play out their own piece of amazing aviation history. The 17th Recon had been sent to attack the Samah Airdrome on Hainan Island and got a nasty surprise - the cliffs overlooking the field had AA guns where there weren't supposed to be any which began firing downward into the squadron on their attack run. Additionally the Japanese fighters were up in the air and waiting for them. While strafing the airdrome and it's installations Goodrich's plane was seriously hit by anti-aircraft fire and had it's right stabilizer and rudder completely shot off. Additionally the fuselage and wings were holed in a number of places. Les Meyers, manning the tail guns at the time, suffered shrapnel wounds, as did George B Carr, waist gunner. If that weren't enough, as Goodrich turned his crippled plane out to sea, sixteen Japanese fighters attacked the squadron, four of them zeroing in on Goodrich's B-25. Sgt. Les Meyer's had his hands full with two Zero's attacking from the rear 5 o'clock position, and with only one of his two .50's was still operating fired three twenty-round bursts into the first attacker as he closed within 300 yards, hitting the engine and cockpit area - the plane started pouring smoke and dove into a spin. He recalled it 55 years later in his unassuming way: *"...we came down off the ocean and down into the airbase there and at the time they didn't know where the rest of Jap navy was and there they were sitting in the middle of the bay when we came down through. Of course we came down low. We had Jap planes come after us, and I got lucky and managed to shoot one down, even though I was, you know, hurt. That was just one of those things..."* Les did not follow the first Zero as it crashed, instead he turned his guns on the second Zero but to his relief the second plane had been scared off by the top turret's guns. He was officially credited with the kill on the confirmation of Sgt. Eugene Oterson, the top turret gunner, who saw the plane go in.

With the attackers fought off, Goodrich then proceeded to complete one of the more amazing feats of piloting of the war. He pulled up alongside Kilgore's plane and started flying formation, just as if his plane was perfectly fine. He then managed to somehow fly his crippled B-25 across the wide expanse of the China Sea some 700 miles and safely land the plane at Lingayen without any further injury to his crew. He was the last one to land and according to George Robinson who was standing there at the time Goodrich actually buzzed the airstrip (indicating an aerial victory) before setting down. I can only surmise that the wounded crewmen weren't that serious. The 17th Recon historian who was there at the time was at a complete loss to explain how Goodrich accomplished his feat.

Having been alerted by radio in advance, two Mitchell Reps had come up from Manila to witness the plane land. One of the technical inspectors came up and told Goodrich in a very official manner that the B-25 was absolutely not flyable, to which Goodrich caustically replied: "It's fortunate that I wasn't aware of that fact after we left the target."

(Below) Too close for comfort - Lt. Goodrich's B25 sans rudder and stabilizer after his remarkable feat piloting the crippled plane to an emergency landing at Lingayen. Note the additional damage near the waist gunners position. I spoke with Les Meyers in 2000 and he was very nonchalant when asked about how he still managed to shoot down a plane after being wounded: ""Yeah. That (AA) fire that took the tail off. There was a piece of plexiglass... I still have that in my leg. They said it was too close to the bone to take out and they said it wouldn't hurt or anything so, it's still there. After 55 years...well I can still walk around anyhow" (Courtesy of Lester Meyers)

(Above) *Goodrich's crew, probably shot in Brisbane. Top row left to right: Lester Meyers (Tail Gunner), George B. Carr (radio operator), Eugene Oterson (engineer). Bottom row L- R M.V Catlin (co-pilot), Bill R. Carter (navigator) and William S. Goodrich (Pilot). When asked how Goodrich managed to fly the plane with half the tail shot off, George Robinson, who was flying alongside in Kilgore's plane, answered "He flew it in formation! He pulled right up on our left wing. I called Kilgore and Kilgore told him to get off of there. He was flying it well. He was flying it like nothing was wrong with it."* (Courtesy of Lester Meyers)

(Right) *Map of Hainan Island off the south China coast. George C. Robinson, radio operator in Lt. Kilgore's crew, recalled that they didn't have current maps of the island and were given an old National Geographic map for the mission - talk about winging it!*

Map Source: General Drafting Co, Inc.

A Charmin' Lady falls

By May of 1945 Japanese air resistance in the Philippines had been pretty much completely neutralized, but flying combat missions still had plenty of risks. On May 18th, on what seemed a somewhat routine ground support mission against Japanese ground positions against Japanese troops in the Divisoria area Lieutenant Kluth's plane, having had a bomb hang up on the first pass, was making a second pass on the small bario of about 20 houses when it was hit by ground fire, causing a fire to break out in the right engine. Flying at 250 Mph and at low altitude she quickly crash landed, breaking in two and leaving a debris trail nearly three quarters of a mile long.

Miraculously, the other circling 17th Recon planes spotted two crewmen standing by the downed plane and Sgt. George Robinson ejected their life raft with supplies near the crash site hoping it might be of help. It turned out that Sgt. Harold Ford, the turret gunner, survived the crash relatively intact, as did Lt Kluth and co-pilot Lt. Young, although the latter two were both wounded. The two standing crew that were spotted was Sgt. Ford helping Lt. Kluth. The other three crew had died in the crash. Sgt Ford's account of the crash was thus: *"Just as I got off the turret seat we hit the ground. I grabbed hold of the armor plate to support myself but believe that I was knocked out by the crash for the next I remember I was wedged in the back with my foot caught on something. I had to remove my shoe to release my foot after which I crawled out of the airplane. I called for Sergeant Hawk and much to my surprise as I looked around I was separate from the rest of the wrecked airplane. The tail had broken completely off when we crashed."*

Ford located and pulled Lt Kluth, who's shirt was burned off, out of the cockpit and laid him on the wing where he gave him a shot of morphine He then extracted co-pilot Lt. Young from the plane and administered first aid as well. Both Kluth and Young had serious burns and cuts but Kluth seemed like he might make it. Young was in bad shape but conscious and asking about the other crew. Hawk (navigator) and Pete Rice (Tail Gunner) had been killed outright in the crash. Very shortly guerrillas of the Philippine Army showed up and told Ford he had to clear out of there pronto as Japanese soldiers were already out looking for them. The guerrillas hustled him off with the Japanese soldiers hot on their tails. Kluth and Young were taken away seperately on makeshift stretchers. Hiding in the hills, Kluth and Young succumbed to their injuries the following morning despite getting medical attention from a Filippino doctor. Sgt Ford was picked up by some Rangers who kept the pursuing Japanese soldiers and their dogs off track by setting various booby traps. Ford managed to make it back to the 17th Base at Lingayen intact after a harrowing five day escape through the mountains and gave a full account of what happened.

(Above) *Major Kluth's plane at Lingayen, Philippines. In the back far right is 17th Recon operations officer Capt. Bert Sill. In less than a month Kluth and four of his crew would be dead and this aircraft would be just scattered wreckage across the Philippine countryside. On May 10th, John flew along with Kluth's crew as a photographer on a mission to Formosa which may explain why this photo was in his collection. That May 10th mission would be the last John would fly in the war and I can only speculate if this incident had anything to do with that.* (John Stava Collection)

(Opposite Page) *Aerial view of Divisoria in the Cagayan Valley on Luzon where a a few traces of smoke marks the final resting place(s) of Charmin' Lady and two of her crew. Kluth and Young would be buried somewhere in the hills beyond the following morning. General Yamashita was hiding his tanks in haystacks in the area and the 17th went in to smoke them out.* (Photo courtesy of Walter Ken Barber)

(Below left) *Another view of the Lady at Lingayen, Philippines, showing the later war 17th Recon markings on her tail rudders which was a variation on the official 5th Air Force logo - the five stars of the Southern Cross with the comet representing the 5th. Major Kluth was a commercial artist by trade and painted many of the nose art on the 17th's air-craft including, presumably, the "Lady".* (Photo courtesy of Walter Ken Barber)

(Below right) *Lt. Walter Ken Barber (center) with two of his ground crew pose in front of his unnamed B-25. Ken Barber was behind Kluth's B-25 the day Charmin' Lady went down. His first mission with the 17th was in early January 1945 to pick up Jene Haehnel back at Tacloban (who survived the Dec. 26th Ditching) and bring him back to Mindoro. Barber retired from the USAF as a Lt. Colonel and lives in California.* (Photo courtesy of Walter Ken Barber)

"...we combat veterans dare not let their memory fade, for God help a nation which forgets it's war dead"

-Garrett Middlebrook, Air Combat at 20 Feet

John Stava Collection

Soldiers and Sailors Momument, Market Street, Sydey.

18309

Army of the United States

RECEIVED FOR RECORD
NOV 26 1945
DONALD F. LY[illegible]
COUNTY RECORDER
CUYA[illegible] COUNTY, [illegible]

VOL 53 PAGE 560

Honorable Discharge

This is to certify that

JOHN H STAVA 15 014 630 Technical Sergeant

17th Reconnaissance Squadron B

Army of the United States

is hereby Honorably Discharged from the military service of the United States of America.

This certificate is awarded as a testimonial of Honest and Faithful Service to this country.

Given at SEPARATION CENTER
Ft Logan Colo

Date 22 September 1945

Kenneth F Goodall

KENNETH F GOODALL
Major Air Corp

Afterword

So here we are at the end of our story. I struggled for quite some time in deciding just how to wrap up this book and in the eleventh hour before firing the finished draft off to the publishers the answer came - not surprisingly - from my uncle John himself, in the form of a letter he wrote sixty years ago, that found itself delivered in my mailbox just last week.

This book has been a lengthy exercise in improbable coincidences. Detailing them would be a book in itself so I'll leave you with this last one, which involved a last minute look through my uncles address book which yielded George "Red" Robinson, who served with my uncle in the 17th Recon and whom, in the course my last minute interviews with him, discovered he still had a letter written to him by my uncle John just after the war. As of this writing George is 89 years old and sharp as a whip and pulling dates and events out of the air sixty-one years later like they happened yesterday. He was the only veteran I spoke with that had correspondence from my uncle, despite the fact they weren't overly well acquainted.

I think it's fair to say this is how my uncle would want me to leave things; after two years, two months and twenty-two days in the Southwest Pacific he's finally made it back to the states intact, his "150 Points" nearly double the average requirement. He's returned home to Cleveland, Ohio to get his bearings, readjust to civilian life and try to figure out what he will do next. WWII is over. And like many surviving vets, I'm guessing that for the first time in a long time he has the luxury of thinking about the future. A new car is on the way, he's looking to move to Denver and here he is writing on New Years Day, 1946, reaching out to a fellow veteran:

January 1, 1946

Hello George,

I can see you enjoy being a civilian again and I'm glad you all got back in good shape. Don't you remember - Kilgore often said he was going to try to stay in the Army. That may explain why he is not home. I arrived in San Francisco the night of July 4th but didn't get out of the army until September 22nd. By that time I got orders for a couple more oak leaf clusters and battle stars so I wound up with 150 points. What delayed me some was an attack of malaria which left me in the hospital for a while and still pops up in me once in awhile.

I'm not working yet. For several reasons I want to live in Denver so no point in looking for a job here. I'm just visiting my family and sweating out delivery of a new car which should arrive this month. When it comes I'll be on my way to Denver and a job I hope. It's a bout time I get to work.

Ed Bender and I returned together and caught up with Carter in Frisco. Haven't seen anyone else but did get a card from Cottman. I suppose he's back in the gas business again. I wonder if John Ciallella or any of my old tent mates tried to bring our dog "Cosmo" back?

Let's keep in touch Red. When I'm located in Denver I'll send you my address and sooner or later I'll be going down to Mexico. When that time comes I'll stop in Port Arthur and say hello and meet Evelyne.

Johnny

He did find a job in Denver - serving with the Civil Air Patrol as a photographer from 1948-53, and he did get down to Port Arthur by the way, and did get to meet Evelyne, who still remembers him to this day.

(Opposite Page) *The slip of paper many a combat serviceman longs to see - his discharge papers.* (John Stava Collection)

(Below) *John's letter to George Robinson. Special thanks to George's wife who hung on to this letter for so many years* (courtesy of George Robinson)

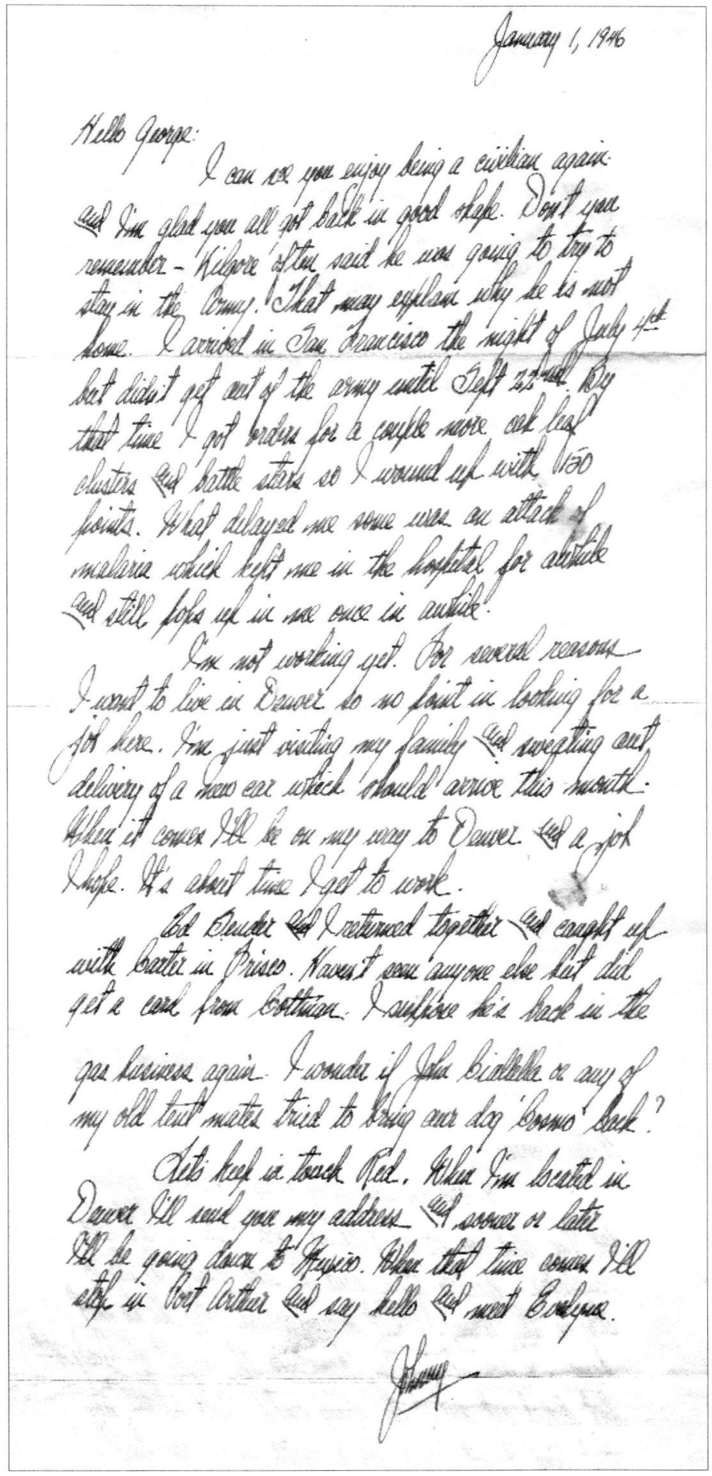

Bibliography and Suggested reading

A variety of sources were drawn from in writing this book. To really understand the scope and depth of the 5th Air Force and the war in the Southwest Pacific during WWII I highly recommend the books and resources listed below. Most will require a bit of investigation on your part as very few books on the 5th Air Force can be found at your local bookstore - but online resellers like Amazon.com and ebay will often turn up reasonable deals on many of these titles. Of course a wealthy amount of information is at your fingertips by simply searching on the web.

PUBLICATIONS:

Alcorn, John S., *The Jolly Rogers - History of the 90th Bomb Group During World War II* California, Historical Aviation Album, 1981
Birdsall, Steve, *Flying Buccaneers*, New York, Doubleday, 1977
Bozung, Jack H. (Editor), *The 5th Over the Southwest Pacific* Los Angeles, AAF Publications Company, 1945?
Claringbold, Michael J., *The Forgotten Fifth*, Australia, Aerothentic Publications, 1999
Dorr, Robert F., *B-24 Liberator Units of The Pacific War,* Great Britain, Osprey Publishing, 1999
Emanual, Cedric, *Southwest Pacific Sketchbook* New York, Prentice-Hall, Inc., 1945
Ethell, Jeffrey L. & Bodie, Warren M., *WWII Pacific War Eagles in Original Color,* Virginia, Widewing Publications, 1997
Ferguson, Max, *Bats Outa Hell Over Biak*, Charleston, Illinois, 1991
Gallagher, James P., *With The Fifth Army Air Force,* Maryland, John Hopkins University Press, 2001
Henebry, John P., *The Grim Reapers At Work in the Pacific Theate - The Third Attack Group of the U.S. Fifth Air Force,* Montana, Pictoral Histories Publishing Company, Inc., 2002
Hickey, Lawrence J., *Warpath Across the Pacific*, Colorado, International Research and Publishing Corporation, 1984, 1996
Hough, Capt. Donald & Arnold, Capt. Elliott, *Big Distance,* New York, Duell, Sloan and Pearce, 1945
Impact: The Army Air Forces' "Confidential Picture History of World War II" Volumes 1-8, James Parton and Company, 1980
Kenney, George C. *General Kenney Reports*, New York, Duell, Sloan and Pearce, 1949
Lambert, John W., *Low Level Attack: Pacific,* Minnesota, Specialty Press, 1997
Lord, Andrew M. Lord, *Tales of the Jolly Rogers,* California, Published by Andrew M. Lord, 1985
McAulay, Lex, *Into The Dragon's Jaws - The Fifth Air Force Over Rabaul*, Arizona, Champlin Fighter Museum Press, 1986
McAulay, Lex, *MacArthur's Eagles - The U.S. Air War Over New Guinea 1943-1944*, U.S.A., Naval Institute Press, 2004
McDowell, Ernest R., *B-25 Mitchell in Action,* Texas, Squadron/Signal Oublications, Inc., 1978
Middlebrook, Garrett *Air Combat At 20 feet*, Fort Worth, Texas, The Global Group, 1989
Rust, Kenn C., *Fifth Air Force Story*, California, Historical Aviation Album, 1973
Sakaida, Henry, *Aces of the Rising Sun,* Illinois, Osprey, 2002
Sinton, Russell (Editor), *The Menace From Moresby*, (Reprint) Nashville, Battery Press, 1989
Sturtzebecker, Russell, *The Roarin' 20's*, Kennett Square, Pennsylvania, KNA Press, Inc, 1976
The Best Damn Heavy Bomber Unit in the World - The Jolly Rogers, Sydney, John Sands Pty. Ltd., 1944
Turner Publishing Company, *Fifth Air Force*, Kentucky, Turner Publishing Company 1991
Warpath - Story of the 345th Bombardment Group in WWII, (Reprint of Original Squadron History) Penn., Schiffer Publishing Ltd., 1997

WEBSITES:

www.aerothentic.com *Michael Claringbolds invaluable resource on the 5th Air Force*
www.sunsetters38bg.com *Website for the 38th Bomber Group*
www.90thbombgroup.org *Website for the 90th Bomber Group "Jolly Rogers"*
www.redraiders22bg.com *Website for the 22nd Bomber Group "Red Raiders"*
web.cortland.edu/van/345thBombGroup.htm *Homepage For the 345th Bomber Group "Air Apaches"*
www.pacificwrecks.com *Justin Taylan's excellent source of 5th AF info*
home.st.net.au/~dunn/5thaf.htm *Peter Dunne's massive website covering every aspect the war in the SW Pacific*
http://8thattacksqdnassoc.tripod.com/WWIIa.html *Website for the 3rd Bomber Group, 8th Bomber Squadron*
http://www.adamsplanes.com/ *Interesting tidbits on the 345th BG including interviews.*

Contributors

Of course the real meat and bones of this book came from talking with the veteran's themselves, in addition to families, friends and various authors and historians. The bulk of information and photographs in this book came from John Stava himself and his own personal papers (Citation reports, etc) but this project would have been impossible if not for the help of the following people:

5th AF & WWII Veterans:

Walter Ken Barber - Pilot, 17th Reconnaissance Squadron - *Phone interview and correspondance 2005-6*
Carl R. Camp - Gunner, 90th Bomber Group - *Phone interviews & Correspondance 2006, 2007*
George B. Carr - Gunner, 17th Reconnaissance Squadron - *Phone interview 1999*
Robert Crowe - 5th AF Advon Photo Lab *Phone interview 1999*
Lynn Daker - Pilot, 345th Bomber Group, 500th BS - *Correspondance 2006*
Walt Davis - Gunner, 17th Reconnaissance Squadron - *Correspondance 1999*
Ken Gastgeb - HQ, 345th Bomber Group - *Correspondance 2006*
Bill Gelvin - Pilot, 17th Reconnaissance Squadron - *Correspondance 1999*
Jack Heyn - Photographer, 3rd Bomber Group - *Correspondance 2000-2007*
Harold D. Hilderman - Pilot, 17th Reconnaissance Squadron - *Phone interview 1999*
Frederick H. Hill - Photographer, 71st Tactical Recon Group - *Correspondance 2000-2006*
Kenny King - Ableseaman, Royal Australian Navy (HMS Manunda) - *Assorted Conversations 1999-2003*
Lester R. Meyers - Gunner, 17th Reconnaissance Squadron - *Phone interviews and correspondance 1999 - 2000*
Garrett Middlebrook - Pilot, 38th BG - *Phone Interviews and correspondance 2000 - 2006*
Fred Miller - 5th AF Advon Photo Lab *Phone interviews 1999, 2005-6*
George C. Robinson - Radio Operator, 17th Reconnaissance Squadron - *Phone interviews and correspondance 2006*
Ray Smeltzer - Gunner, 90th Bomber Group - *Correspondance 1999-2000*
Russell Sturzebecker - Pilot, 320th BG - *Phone Interview 1998*
Vic Tatelman - Pilot, 345th Bomber Group, 499th BS - *Correspondance 2006 - 2007*

Family and Friends of 5th AF Veterans:

Josephine Stava - sister of John Stava - *Conversations 1993-1994*
Connie Stava - widow of John Stava - *Conversations & correspondance 1993-1994*
Marge Bong Drucker - widow of Major Richard I Bong - *Phone interviews and correspondance 1999-2001*
Marc Wiederwax - son of Dick Wiederwax, 5th Advon Photo Lab - *Correspondance 1999-2006*
Richard Cavenaugh - son of Robert Cavenaugh, 17th Reconnaissance Squadron - *Correspondance 2002*
Elaine and Barry Kasmer - Elaine is the daughter of Jerome Schrenk, 22nd BG Photographer - *Correspondance 2006*

The following Authors and Historians provided invaluable information on the 5th Air Force as well as on specific planes and personnel:

Peter Dunn - webmaster of "Oz at war"
Michael J. Claringbold - Author and Historian
Lex McAuley - Author and Historian
Ian Quinn - British Airways Pilot in SE asia & local historian
Barry Spink - Maxwell AFB Archivist & researcher
Yvonne Kincaid - National Archives and Records Administration
Paul Van Valkenburg - Historian, 345th Bomber Group
Bob Ford and Gary Gray, 90th Bomb Group Association

In addition to assorted Mission Reports, Flight Rosters and photos that were accessed in the National Archives at College Park the following microfilm reels from Maxwell Air Force Base were also referenced:

B0300 345th Bomber Group Squadron Histories 1944-45
B0782 71st Tac Recon History 1944-45
A0907 17th Recon History 1944-45

Acknowledgements

Over the last ten years a lot of people gave invaluable assistance and were instrumental in pulling this whole project off. First I have to thank, of course, my uncle John Stava, who better or for worse undertook the experiences and documented them upon which this book is built. Next would be my aunt Josephine, who kept all his photos and documents in safekeeping for fifty some odd years, and then her cousin Willie Linsky who after inheriting these materials very generously and unflinchingly handed them over to me, without which this project never would have materialized. The mysterious Mrs Oscar Walther of Colorado who hung on to all my uncles papers and photos for many years after he disappeared from there, ultimately packing them up and sending them off to the Air Force with instructions to send them to his last known address - which turned out to be my great Aunt's. Next in order I have to thank all of the 5th Air Force veteran's who shared their direct personal experiences that gave this project it's flesh and bones as well as shedding light on who my uncle was and what he exactly did, information impossible to glean from impersonal mission reports and historical accounts. A few who need to specifically thanked are; Bob Crowe and Fred Miller for helping me understand who and what the 5th AF Advon Photo Section was and what they did, Jack Heyn, The unofficial "Mayor of Des Moines" for his insights as a photographer in the Pacific and for unflinchingly agreeing to write the forward to this book as well as his stimulating rants and raves that continue to appear in my e-mail inbox, Les Meyers for his photos and accounts of the 17th Recon, Walter Ken Barber for ultimately providing the last anecdote of this book and thus drawing my attention to my uncles last mission, George Robinson for still recalling such lurid details about the 17th Recon after so many years and never letting me off the phone without at least one or two excellent stories. Marc Wiederwax for providing most of his fathers photo collection which fleshed out a good part of this book. Carl Camp for his unflinching candidness, tenacious love and curiousity of everything in life and providing crucial details on the mission to Woleai. Australian authors and historians Michael J. Claringbold and Lex McAuley who unselfishly gave detailed feedback on my errant questions and of course the ever vigilant historians at NARA and Maxwell Air Force Base. My father Reid who unwittingly fired my interest from a young age in WWII aviation history, my uncle Shim who inspired my sense of no holds barred research and the abundant opportunities at the National Archives, my sister Susan for her photography and input as a professional photojournalist, my Mother and stepfather, Bob, for their patience and understanding of my absence at family events as the deadline drew near, and last my wife Tomiko for her frank insights into Japanese culture and unwavering support over long hours and late nights.

Photo: Susan Stava

ABOUT THE AUTHOR

Robert Stava is the Creative Director of 3d Media Group at Arup, an U.K. based design firm, where his department creates 3d architectural visualizations and animations for a variety of international and private clients. His background is in Advertising and Fine Arts. He's worked at both Young & Rubicam N.Y. and J. Walter Thompson as a designer and later Art Director, and currently his focus is in keeping his 3d visualization group on the cutting edge of the design visualization industry.

He is also a musician who performed with his own band on the alternative New York music scene for over 8 years, an avid New York Times Crossword fanatic and he also trains in traditional style Japanese Karate under Grandmaster Kaicho Nakamura at Seido (Honbu) in N.Y.C..

In addition to his great uncle John, he had two other uncles who served in the Pacific, Fred Burns, a photographer with the 12th Air Force (North Africa, China-Burma theater) and Fred Hodgson of the 34th Engineers (Pearl Harbor, Saipan).

Originally from Cleveland, Ohio, Stava grew up in upstate New York. He now lives in Park Slope, Brooklyn with his wife, Tomiko, a professional Ballet dancer and teacher, their Siberian Husky and a cat. This is his first publication as both a writer and designer. He is currently at work on his next book, a colloberation with Carl Camp covering his experiences as a B-24 gunner in the 90th Bomb Group in New Guinea during World War II.